The Garage Sale Gal's
Guide to Making Money
Off Your Stuff

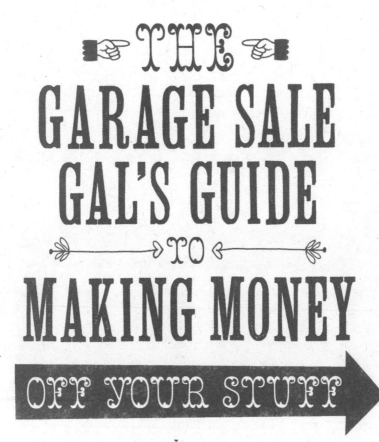

THE GARAGE SALE GAL'S GUIDE TO MAKING MONEY OFF YOUR STUFF

by

LYNDA HAMMOND

GIBBS SMITH
TO ENRICH AND INSPIRE HUMANKIND

First Edition
15 14 13 12 11   5 4 3 2 1

Published by
Gibbs Smith
P.O. Box 667
Layton, Utah 84041

1.800.835.4993 orders
www.gibbs-smith.com

Designed by Sugar
Cover Illustration by Alison Oliver
Printed and bound in Canada

Gibbs Smith books are printed on either recycled, 100% post-consumer waste,
FSC-certified papers or on paper produced from sustainable PEFC-certified
forest/controlled wood source. Learn more at www.pefc.org.

Library of Congress Cataloging-in-Publication Data

Hammond, Lynda.
  The garage sale gal's guide to making money off your stuff
/ Lynda Hammond. – 1st ed.
       p. cm.
  ISBN 978-1-4236-2099-0
  1. Garage sales. I. Title.
  HF5482.3.H36 2011
  658.8'7–dc22

                                        2010049015

This book is dedicated to the two people who took me garage saling that first time in Kansas—my sister in-law, Colleen Nunn, whose faith, love, support, and kindness encourages me and everyone who knows her, and Colleen's mother, Kathleen Frisbie, who convinced me to write a book when she told me, "You need to document this. Write down the stories of how you found all of these wonderful things at garage sales."

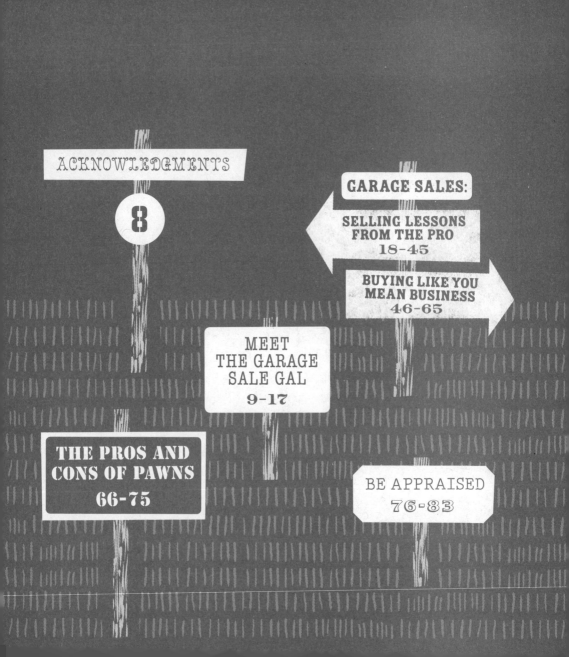

☞ CONTENTS

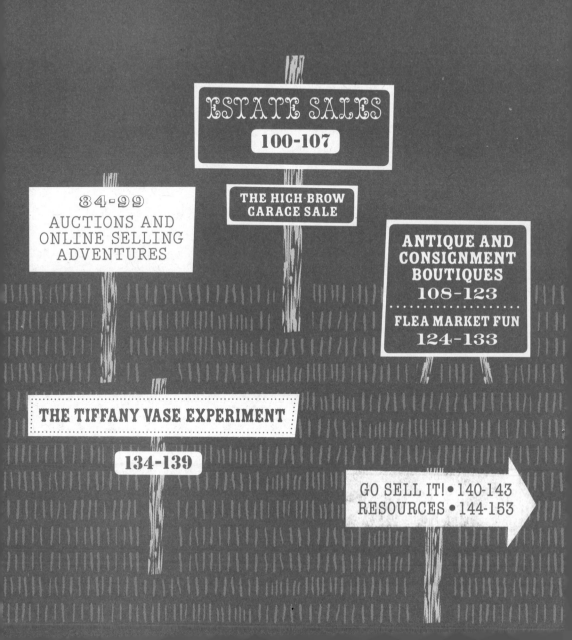

ACKNOWLEDGMENTS

Even though putting words to a page is a solitary task, writing a book takes a lot of support. I want to thank the people who cheered me on along the way. Thank you to my husband, Kevin Nunn, who helped me to turn off the *I Love Lucy* reruns and get started; Jim Wambold, for his patience and expertise; Kent Nunn, for his ability to read between the lines; newspaper editor, Dan Shearer, who gave me my start at the *Arizona Republic*; Paul Maryniak, the *Republic's* community editor, who allows me to continue having a blast writing my weekly garage sale column; Suzanne Taylor, associate publisher of Gibbs Smith, who believed in me and gave me a chance; and Michelle Branson, Gibbs Smith associate editor, for guiding me along the way. Kudos to Sandra Shea, to whom I still owe a dinner, and Amy McDonald, my friend since our days on Eastmoor Boulevard. I also want to mention my parents, Phyllis and Jerry Brinkman, who, thanks to all their accolades and compliments, though perhaps a bit biased, give me the confidence to write every single day, even if I don't feel like it. And lastly, to my grandmother, Minerva Sweet, who is never far from my heart and thoughts. Mercy me, Grandma would've loved this book!

MEET THE GARAGE SALE GAL

My name is Lynda and I am a bargain hunter. In this book you'll learn ways to make the most money off your stuff—things you have gathering dust in your closet, your attic, or your garage. Whether you're selling online, in antique or consignment stores, pawn shops, or from your own driveway, this book can help. Living frugally and knowing how, what, and where to sell things can be a lifesaver. It has been for me, and learning it started at an early age.

When I was growing up in Columbus, Ohio, we didn't have much money. Mom raised me and my two older brothers alone on a secretary's salary. I learned that I had to respect and work for money. I earned cash by going door to door, up and down Eastmoor Boulevard, looking for odd jobs. I would wash dishes, clean out cupboards, rake leaves, and shovel snow for about $2.

I was ten years old when I walked two miles to the bank next to the Super Duper Grocery Store and opened my first savings account with a baby food jar full of quarters.

For birthdays and for Christmas, my grandma gave us rolls of coins; and off to the bank I'd go. I'm still programmed to pick up a penny whenever I see it—I'm so determined that I'll inadvertently stop traffic on a busy sidewalk to bend down and pick it up. Embarrassed? Me? Hardly!

My point is that small change you find between the sofa cushions—something we may ignore or take for granted—can make a big difference in your life. While at the same time, some of the stuff you have sitting around your house—things you don't need or want, a Roseville pottery planter, costume jewelry from your mom, or maybe a toy you had as a kid, can also lead to a lot of jars full of quarters.

Thanks to babysitting jobs, I eventually began taking dollar bills to the bank. That money helped put me through college. In 1985, I graduated from The Ohio State University with a degree in broadcast journalism. Soon I landed a news reporter's position at the CBS affiliate, KDLH-TV in freezing but beautiful Duluth, Minnesota, where I continued on the path of frugal living—I had to on my annual $10,800 salary! For almost fifteen years, I hop-scotched across the country living the dream and working my way up to the coveted position of news anchor.

In 1997, the "cushy" life for me all came crashing down when I lost my anchoring position at a station in Kentucky. It was a good gig and I'd been there three years—gosh I thought things we're going along swimmingly. But management wanted to go a "different direction." I was devastated. Television news was the only thing I knew how to do, or so I thought.

Just three months later, my husband, Kevin, who was also in television news, got a news director's position at WXIN-TV in Indianapolis. We both happily made the move, but when a job in television for me never materialized, I spiraled into depression, filling my time by making sugar cookies (and eating them) and sitting on the couch watching old black-and-white who-dun-it movies.

The one thing that did take my mind off the job search (or lack thereof) was the new house we were building. We had moved so often that we didn't have a lot of furniture or tchotchkes for decorating. Those childhood lessons of working hard and spending little came racing back. No, I didn't go door to door looking for odd jobs, but I did go from garage sale to garage sale making bargain buys—it beat paying retail at furniture stores. I ended up decorating the entire house using garage sale finds. The funny thing is, just a few years before, you would have been hard pressed to find me anywhere near a garage sale, let alone at one.

After four years, another blow. Kevin lost his job at the station when new management took over. We tried to get jobs to make ends meet but no one would hire us, saying we were over qualified. Two months later, on September 11, 2001, the world changed. The terrorist attacks on the United States caused heartache and havoc. The economy weakened as people, fearing another attack, opted to stay home rather than travel. People were laid off and jobs were scarce.

Thank goodness for garage sales. To make ends meet, Kevin and I would buy something—say an old vase—for $1, and sell it in online auctions for $20. We paid the house payment and bills for three months this way. Eventually, in 2002, both Kevin and I got jobs in Arizona—Kevin with the Associated Press and me at ABC 15 as a fill-in health reporter, producer—a temporary job filling in for a woman on maternity leave.

After losing my job that time in Kentucky, I had a one-track mind. All I wanted was to be back in the business; but it was one of those be-careful-what-you-wish-for things, because once I got back into a busy and hectic newsroom, I wanted out. I had lost the fire. Instead, I came up with a way to turn my garage saling passion into more than just a hobby.

It was scary leaving television news for good and embarking on a new challenge, especially for a "career" in garage saling.

continued on page 16

MY FIRST GARAGE SALE

➤➤➤ I was a garage-sale snob. The thought of rummaging through or buying something used by someone else was...well, icky, and certainly not my idea of fun. Now, don't get me wrong, I love to shop. But back then the closest I got to "icky" was sticky when I spilled part of my tall, non-fat, triple-shot latte on my Neiman's credit card while I was on a spending spree. Buying things from someone's driveway with—gasp—hand-me-downs hanging from a makeshift clothesline suspended between a mailbox and a porch railing wasn't even on my radar.

It was in Salina, a town right smack in the middle of Kansas, back in 1992, when something profound happened. I went to my first garage sale. I was visiting relatives and they dragged me along. My sister-in-law, Colleen, and her mother, Kathleen, are lifelong garage sale enthusiasts and search for treasures any chance they get.

I remember everything about that beautiful spring day. It was the kind of day where the sky was blue, there wasn't a cloud in sight, and the cold winter air was giving way to warmer temperatures. We made a turn into an upscale neighborhood where a sign pointed to a sale. Before the car stopped I saw it. Although its finish was dull, it glistened in the sunshine and beckoned me. "It" was a big old copper boiler, the kind your grandma might have used for cooking and cleaning. I could just picture it spicing up a bare spot in my kitchen. And that's when it happened. I, a bargain-buying snob, negotiated my first garage sale purchase. I might have been green at this garage sale stuff, but I wasn't shy. The man wanted $50, but I talked him down to $30. He said he wasn't sure why he was selling it, that it had been his grandmother's, and he had always loved that copper boiler. He nearly talked himself out of selling it to me. But I gave him the money and he took it, though a bit reluctantly. I walked away excitedly because I had just purchased my first garage sale item. But I also felt a little guilty that I had taken his precious childhood memory—so I walked faster! I was hooked.

After pondering several ideas which included driving bargain hunters in an old school bus from sale to sale—and that wouldn't have been pretty since I don't know how to drive a bus—I came up with a plan to help put garage saling where I think it belongs, in mainstream media. In 2004, I started my website, www.GarageSaleGal.com as a portal for garage sale enthusiasts. I also went back to television—not as an anchor—but as the Garage Sale Gal. I began appearing on Phoenix TV stations as the expert on garage saling, while at the same time promoting my website. And get this; I even became a teacher. I taught courses on garage sale buying and selling at Mesa Community College in Arizona. I also took my passion to print media by writing three sample Garage Sale Gal columns for *The Arizona Republic*, the primary newspaper in Phoenix and the state. My editor had his doubts, saying, "We're going to give you a shot, but I don't know what you'll be writing about in six weeks." Years later, and at nearly 300 columns and counting, I still haven't run out of people, garage sales, and treasures to write about. This is a testament today to the popularity of garage sales. Everyone has a story and wants to share it.

Whether you're buying, selling, exploring, just browsing, or maybe even looking for a new career, I hope you'll find this book informative, eye-opening, and entertaining. So before you start your next bargain hunting adventure, read *The Garage Sale Gal's Guide to Making Money Off Your Stuff*. And, good luck!

1

GARAGE SALES

Selling Lessons From The Pro

Holding a garage or yard sale is probably the single easiest and most effective way to bring in cash fast. There's no overhead, no one to pay, and it can be held at your convenience, and best of all, at your own house. And the feeling you get when you have freed up space in your home and made money is one of relief, control, and even pure happiness.

PURGING

The process of purging is the first step toward having a sale. Clutter can be overwhelming so start slowly by cleaning out a cupboard or drawer. Choose a staging area in the garage or basement and each time you find something you don't want, put it in this designated area. I know a family that has a roped off section in their garage in Scottsdale, Arizona, for this very purpose. All year long whenever they find something to sell, it gets put in the pile for the next sale.

As you're sorting—look at things closely. It would be awful if you sold that jewelry box for a $1 and later remembered you had hidden a wedding ring in it. In the spring of 2009, a woman in Israel bought a new mattress as a surprise for her elderly mother and threw away the old one. But ouch! The bigger surprise was that her mother had stashed her life savings in the mattress—a million dollars! The story may seem unbelievable, but the Associated Press and other news organizations around the globe ran the report. Police in Tel Aviv even secured landfills as they were searched for the "stuffed" mattress. Although some may question the accuracy of this report, one thing that's certainly

 **Seller beware—check everything—clothes pockets, purses, wallets, boxes, trunks, suitcases, and anything and everything else you can think of.**

true is that the thought of losing something valuable simply because you forgot about it makes you weak in the knees, doesn't it?

I'll never forget going to a garage sale in Higley, Arizona, where Brent and his family were getting rid of some stuff. During a lull in activity Brent looked inside some of the merchandise for sale, including a purse. He got quite a surprise. His wife had left seven credit cards inside—older ones but still open and active. "I'm really lucky I found this. I mean it had been sitting out here for sale for three hours," Brent told me minutes after finding the stocked purse.

And in another case, a buyer did get away with quite a stash but didn't know it. Diane found a new container of L'eggs Panty Hose at a sale—you know the kind of hose that came rolled up in a plastic egg. It was her size so she bought them. One day when she was getting ready for work, she sat down and pulled out her brand new pair of hose—but when she opened the egg—there were no panty hose. Instead, four $20 bills fell out. Diane paid a quarter for the $80! Now, that's some return on your money!

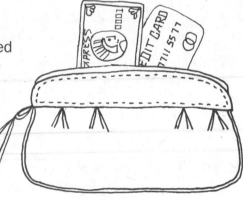

 Sometimes the hardest part about getting rid of your old things are the memories attached to them. This particular hang-up is probably the toughest for me and a big reason clearing the clutter can be so daunting.

WHEN IN DOUBT PUT IT OUT

You never know why someone is buying something or what they'll use it for. At one of my sales, a lady bought my old jeans, not to wear, but instead to transform into purses. I know one man who buys junk at garage sales—literally boxes of miscellaneous nuts and bolts and plastic gizmos. His hobby is fixing stuff, so as he says, "I can use just about anything." Another woman looks for mismatched bone china—even if it's chipped or cracked. She buys it for pennies and takes a hammer to the china (a great stress reliever!) and creates mosaic tile projects. Then there's the guy who bought part of a Halloween costume from me—a single, gory, rubber foot. (The matching foot had melted in our

 To paraphrase a blogger, if you hold on to something for sentimental reasons, you need to realize that selling it doesn't mean you're letting go of the memory. That's helped me to feel a little less guilty about getting rid of things.

garage during the sizzling hot Arizona summer.) I still wonder about that, but I bet he had a good foothold on his plans for it!

PRICELESS

Okay, drum roll please . . . here is my single best tip for making the most money at your garage sale: **Don't price anything!** I know, I know. This advice is often met with resistance. Shaking your head? Rolling your eyes? Are you ready to close this book? Wait. Hear me out. I can explain. Really! Pricing items is the most annoying, tedious, and time-consuming task associated with having a garage sale, and if you can cut out this step you'll save time and make more money. On the pages that follow, I'll show you how to make your sale a "priceless" success. But first, let me warm you up to the idea by sharing a couple of stories.

It was late in the day when a woman pulled up and looked at the leftovers at my garage sale. She picked up a comforter that had a small hole smack dab in the middle. She looked it over, spotted the defect, but wanted it anyway. She asked me the price. I told her, "Oh, it doesn't matter, just name your price."

She said she didn't want to offend me by offering a price too low. I reassured her there would be no offense taken. I saw her pondering. Then she began to speak, hesitantly at first. "Would you take . . . $20 for it?"

Would I?! That turned out to be my best sale of the day.

Now, here's my point; had I priced that blanket, I might have put $5 on it and then, taking into consideration negotiations, I probably would have been lucky to get $3. But by not pricing it, that turned out to be well, priceless.

I have friends, family, and readers of my column who strongly disagree with me on the pricing issue. But these naysayers seem to have one thing in common—they've never tried it.

Lori thought she'd give it a shot. She paid $900 at the store for a table and six chairs, but was ready to get rid of them. She was hoping to get $100. The first customer of the day went for the table set. When he asked the price, Lori got tongue-tied, so he blurted, "I brought $400 with me."

"I felt an immediate adrenaline rush," Lori recalled. "I thought, 'Oh my gosh, we're going to make much more money than we ever thought on just this one thing.' It's so stressful to price things, but now that I know I don't have to, that I can just put stuff out and it'll sell, I'll definitely have another sale again." Lori settled on $300 for the table because she felt guilty taking all of the man's money.

Jack, an avid garage saler just doesn't buy the no-pricing idea. In fact, if the merchandise isn't tagged, he doesn't buy anything.

When he saw one of my columns trumpeting the idea of going priceless, he was angry at me for even suggesting it. "If things aren't priced, I just walk right on by. I'm not going to do the seller's job for them."

PRICING AT AN UN-PRICED SALE

When naming a price on the spot—attitude and state of mind, along with a bit of finesse, all play a key part. Sellers and buyers may see the same items sitting in the driveway but the way they view them can be as different as night and day. Say a 1950s McCoy cookie "house" is perched on a table with no price tag. The seller may think, "I just want to get rid of that old thing." But when the buyer eyes it she can't believe her good fortune. She had been looking for one for years. The cute house with the roof for a lid tugs at the heart strings, recalling the times she'd reach into the cookie jar for one of Grandma's sugared delights. With that pleasant connection to the past, the buyer wants that cookie jar shaped like a house and will likely offer a price higher than the seller would have even considered putting on it. This scenario won't play out every time, but when it does, it will offset any sales you may have lost because things weren't priced.

HAGGLING

Garage salers are frugal and proud of it and if we can succeed at getting a lower price, it's a badge of honor. Buyers feel victorious if the seller comes down in price. Haggling is part of the fun. Gosh, $5 is a great price, but if we can get that antique cake plate for $3, now that's a deal. Remember, garage salers usually don't need what we're buying. Instead, we just like it or the price is too low to pass up—or even better—a combination of the two. It's a hoot to buy a Coach designer handbag at a garage sale for $10, but it wouldn't be the same thrill to pay $80. So sellers should be prepared for the pricing game. Build some wiggle room into your prices. Here's how negotiating should go from a seller's prospective: If you're hoping to get $5 for something, suggest $8. If the buyer then comes back at $5 it's okay to split the difference and get $6. If you have something marked $2, buyers are simply wired to ask if you'll take $1. So quote $3 or $4 in order to settle on $2.

When morning arrives, the sale is set up, and we're having a second cup of coffee waiting for the crowds, the pricing game is just getting started. To make the most money, pay attention.

 **Ask the buyer to name her price. Often times it'll be higher than what you would have marked it. Remember, the buyer wants the item; you want to get rid of it.**

⇛→ One of the first things I do when I see an interesting item is turn it over to check the bottom. I look for the maker's mark and other brand identifiers—I do this in nice restaurants, too. I can't resist cute coffee cups and saucers, but that's another story, maybe even a book on manners! Anyway, sometimes I see the original price tag from the store still attached and—oops—turns out it's lower than what the seller at the garage sale is now asking. Remember, buyers want a deal and if they realize you paid less, they'll put it down faster than they can say "rip off." So, unless the original tag is higher, remove it.

Watch what customers are checking out. If someone is eyeing that old blender, yell out a price—taking into consideration the brand, condition, age, and how badly you want to get rid of it. Consider adding some facts, too. "That's from the 1960s" or "That's a rare Hull planter." Sell it! Buyers often appreciate the extra information and might feel more inclined to pay your asking price if they feel like the item is more "special."

POKER FACE

If a buyer spots an item, picks it up, and walks around with it, that's a "tell," as they say at the poker table. I can "tell" they want it. They've picked it up to claim it, to make sure another customer doesn't grab it. So, quote a higher price.

 Consider the buyer when quoting a price. If a well-dressed woman gets out of her shiny new BMW carrying a Gucci bag (yes, I have seen this) quote a higher price on whatever she picks up. Plan to charge more when you see shoppers arrive in style.

PRICE IF YOU MUST

Ok, so you've heard my side, but if you still feel more comfortable pricing things—no problem. But do this: Don't price anything under a buck. I often see price tags of fifty cents or less on candles, vases, or clothing. Chances are most buyers would pay a buck for a decent unused candle or a barely worn sweatshirt. So, don't undercut yourself on the price.

Consider pricing things by table. Display one with clothes and attach a sign—$2. Load another with toys—$1. This can save you from pricing every single item. One problem—and it's a fairly

If you're firm on the price then you're less likely to get rid of it. It may not seem fair, and sometimes selling your things at garage sales can be frustrating—especially if you paid $1,200 for that television. Well, here's a dose of reality. The buyer doesn't care what the seller paid; she only cares what she's about to pay.

big one—when the sale gets crowded, you may not see from which table an item was grabbed. The buyer may not even notice, either, and you're still forced to come up with a price on the spot. So, is my idea for not pricing items beginning to grow on you?

Going priceless encourages conversation and that's part of the fun. It's more rewarding to purchase things at a sale where the seller is friendly and kind, so talk to your buyers.

THE DAY

The success of your sale also depends on which day, or days, you choose to hold it. Thursdays or Fridays are great for sellers. While Saturday may be the most popular day to hold a sale, it won't be your most profitable.

Reasons Not To Price	Reasons To Price
➡ It's stressful and time-consuming.	➡ You don't have to come up with a price on the spot or talk to buyers.
➡ You'll make more money.	➡ If it's a sale involving multiple sellers, pricing items by using different-colored stickers can help keep profits separate.
➡ Price tags get taken off, blown off, or peeled off.	
➡ Buyers don't see the price tag and ask anyway.	➡ Some buyers will appreciate your efforts to make your sale organized and won't mind paying the marked price.
➡ Pre-printed price stickers cost money— about $8 for 50.	
➡ Thanks to haggling, buyers don't pay the marked price anyway.	➡ And remember, if you do price it and you must have a certain amount to make it worthwhile to sell, be sure to factor in a haggling amount.

A weekday is better because you're getting a jump on the competition. The best way I can help you understand this is by describing a typical scenario. Let's say you are out looking for sales when you come to a street corner on a Friday

morning and see just one garage-sale sign. Chances are you'll go to that one sale. But now, let's say it's Saturday, and there are seven signs at that street corner, each pointing a different direction. Odds are you won't go to all those sales. You'll hit one or two then drift off in another direction never making it back to the place where you started. Or, let's say you do make it to all of those sales. Like any good garage saler, you'll be thrifty by spreading out the money among all the sales, or hanging onto it until something really strikes your fancy. Bottom line, sellers won't make as much money when there are plenty of sales for buyers to choose from. The day of the week that's common for garage sales in your area might be different from mine. When I lived in Indianapolis, Thursdays and Fridays were the big days. So, if you want to get a jump on the competition, determine when most people hold garage sales and set up your shop the day before.

⋙→ Hey, here's something interesting. Did you know there's a designated day for garage sales? The second Saturday in August is National Garage Sale Day. C. Daniel Rhodes of Hoover, Alabama, submitted the idea to Chase's Calendar of Events. "It just seemed like it would be more convenient if we all held it on the same day." Daniel, a real estate appraiser, doesn't actually garage sale much, but he does make the time to go one day a year. "Usually I'll pop in on someone who's having a sale and find out if they know it's National Garage Sale Day. Then I'll buy something and tell them that it was me who created that day."

Weekday sales are always good in part because buyers stop at sales on their way to work or school.

 **Saturday is a buyer's market, whereas Thursdays and Fridays make for a seller's market. Have a sale on a weekday and on a Saturday and compare your profits. You'll likely make twice the amount on the weekday or the first day of your sale. I always do.**

Never have a sale on a Sunday. If I see a garage sale sign on the "day of rest," I drive right on by. Why? I assume the sellers forgot to take their signs down from the day before. Plus, I figure the good stuff has already been sold.

THE TIME

Are you perky in the mornings? Do you get up the second that alarm goes off belting out, "The hills are alive with the sound of music . . . ?" I'm a morning person and I've been known to sing a show tune or two before the sun rises. That trait (or annoyance, if you're the one listening) comes in handy when you're having a sale. Most of the action takes place early. So if you're not a rise-and-shine person, I implore you, do everything you can—for just one day out of the 365 mornings we're blessed with—and get up early! It'll be well worth your time. Bargain hunters are out early and you won't want to miss out on selling stuff to the serious buyers.

Don't shoot down the early birds. The earlier the buyers want to walk off with the seeds I've planted, the giddier I am—and I just might break out in song again. If your sale isn't open early, they'll go down the street to find one that is. I get my best crowds and make the most money between six and eight in the morning. Cock-a-doodle-do!

 **Early birds will show up despite your best efforts to keep them at bay. Just build that into your game plan. If you want to start at seven, advertise your opening time as eight.**

⋙→ When I have a garage sale, I love having my mom and dad come over to help Kevin and me. They usually bring things to sell, too. But saying Mom is not much of a morning person is an understatement. Ouchy, Momma! So, I always promise her a Starbucks vanilla latte and, perhaps, even a light breakfast. She still arrives grouchy, but after the coffee, something to nosh, and a few good customers have come and gone, she comes around. So, bribe your helpers and yourself with treats!

ADVERTISE

It would be awful if—after all the work of putting a sale together—no one showed up. In order to assure a good crowd, get the word out at least a few days ahead of time (if you're planning a huge sale with multiple families, spread the word several weeks ahead of time). Newspaper classifieds are pricey. It'll cost about $50 for one tiny ad. And remember, newspaper circulation is dwindling due to the internet, and that means fewer people will see your ad. Classifieds online are the best places to spread the word. Craigslist.org is a free site where sales can be posted, but it is just a nuts-and-bolts website—just the facts ma'am. I'm partial to www.GarageSaleGal.com (go figure!) for listing and looking for sales and where you can also get helpful tips and read columns about my garage sale adventures. I charge a nominal fee, but this helps keep users honest and accountable. A customer probably won't be playing a prank on someone by listing a sale at someone else's house when in fact there isn't one—which has happened on some sites.

Create a flier to hang on bulletin boards, in grocery stores, and at church. And let it go viral by sending it out online. Include a list of some of the items you'll have for sale. If someone sees a washer/dryer set for $50—just what they need—they'll make plans to be there, early!

SIGNS

Imagine you're on a street corner and hear someone scream. What direction do you look? Probably toward the shriek. So, make your announcements "shout" by creating colorful, eye-catching signs.

Even though you've advertised the sale, you still have to point people in the right direction. The key to making a good sign is color. I use that bright neon poster board from craft or office supply stores. Cut it into smaller pieces no bigger than about 15 inches square— big enough to see, yet small enough to avoid flapping in the wind. Stay away from green, white, black, yellow, cardboard, or even pre-made signs—these colors are tough to see because they tend to blend in with the environment or look more like real estate signs and can go unnoticed.

Don't write too much on your sign. Some include the date, time, address, next of kin, social security number, etc.! Okay, I exaggerate. But no matter how good of a driver we are, we can't read more than a word or two. You need only four letters, "SALE," and an arrow. That's it. If getting to your home takes people around lots of twists and turns into your neighborhood,

Keep It Simple

The easier it is to read, the
more buyers you'll attract.

➡➡

Print clearly and boldly
with a thick black marker.

➡➡

If you have the time,
black paint is even better.

➡➡

Use a thick brush to apply.

➡➡

Stay away from spray paint.
It goes on too faint and messy
and is hard to read.

make several smaller signs with just an arrow directing the way at each fork in the road. (For straight ahead, simply place the arrow in the up position.) Stay consistent with color. If you started with pink poster board, use pink for all your signs, including the arrows. Changing color can confuse buyers and lead them in a different direction—away from your sale.

If I come to a corner and have a choice between a neon pink sign that's neat and easy to read and another that's haphazardly made with paint and pieces of cardboard boxes, you can guess which one I'm drawn to—yep, the sale with the pretty pink sign. If the sign looks good, then a buyer assumes the sale will be worth her time. Consider adding balloons to your signs, too. Do anything to make your signs stand out.

When posting signs, start from the inside out. In other words, hang the first sign at the closest corner to your house, the second sign at the next corner, and so on. When your sign hanger is finished, he'll be at the corner furthest from your house. The reason for this is simple; while someone else is hanging the signs, you could be busy selling items to people showing up from the newly posted signs. If you start opposite

 **Before posting signs, make sure you know the rules of your city, county, or HOA. Some communities don't allow signs while others have restrictions on where you can post them.**

(from the farthest corner out) you won't get any customers until the sign hanger is completely done. And I can guarantee the sign hanger will have a few cars following him. Seriously! I've seen it happen and I've even done it before. Then, when your sale is done for the day, take the signs down farthest from your house first. This will allow you to make a few last sales.

SIGN SITUATIONS

Signs get stolen, blown down, or even covered up by another seller who may point buyers to their sale and away from yours, nasty tactic, but it does happen. Julie found that out the hard way. She put her signs up at six in the morning then opened up shop. But no customers arrived. Turns out her signs had been hijacked. Someone also having a sale that morning posted their signs over Julia's and pointed drivers in a different direction. "Wow. I didn't think about that with the signs. All I thought about was making my sale look presentable with the tables and stuff." Although it sounds like a minor problem, someone else's garage sale sign really can put a damper on your sale by making for a slow day and leaving you with less money in your pocket.

SIGN CHECKER

This means every sale needs what I like to call a "sign checker." This isn't someone who plays checkers near your sign. No, this

continued on page 42

The Big Day

On the day of the sale, think of yourself like
a manager of a store. In essence, that's what
you are. Make sure your store is top notch.

➡ Clean the merchandise.
Keep a few rags nearby
to spiff things up. A
sparkling vase will get
you more money than one
splashed with hardened
water spots.

➡ Make sure your items
don't have an odor. Buyers
will turn their noses up
at dirty, dusty, and smoky
things.

➡ Move merchandise onto
the driveway and lawn. The
more people see from their
cars, the more likely they'll
get out and browse.

➡ Make sure your sale
is bright, lively, and full
of color. Bright hues and
interesting shapes or
textures are eye-catching.
Buyers will want to know
what that huge cowboy is
doing at the sale. Oh, it's a
life-size cardboard cut-out
of John Wayne, for $1? I'll
take it . . . pilgrim.

➡ Make shopping easier
for those of us who hate to
crouch and bend down—get
stuff off the ground and
as close to waist-high as
possible. Use long banquet
tables or improvise
by grabbing a pair of
sawhorses or a couple of
boxes the same height.
Place a piece of plywood or
even a door on top.

➡ Group similar things
together; kitchenware
in one area, clothes in

another, electronics together, and so on. You know—like a store.

➡ Hang up clothes. If you don't have racks, use the bottom of your open garage door. Hang chain link between two surfaces—trees, ladders, or anything else that will work and hang clothes by hooking the hangers into individual links in the chain. I discovered this trick from a woman who started her sale with ten huge garbage bags full of clothing, and by the end of the sale, she had only a few pieces left.

➡ Place bigger items—armoires, couches, chairs—toward the end of the driveway. The buyer may be more likely to buy it if it's easier to load up into their vehicle.

➡ Have an electrical source nearby so folks can try small electronics to make sure they work.

➡ Count on your first customer handing you a $20. Have small bills and coins on hand.

➡ Greet buyers with open arms. Strike up conversations. Be friendly. It goes a long way toward making people feel good. If we feel comfortable, we'll stick around your sale a bit longer and buy more.

➡ Wear name tags—seriously. Ok, it may sound a bit too Pollyanna, but it can be a classy touch. I always see customers searching for the seller. Wear one of those "Hello, my name is" stickers. It'll help alleviate frustration for buyers and speed things up. And you can be sure buyers will remember your sale for the unique touch, and that's always a good thing.

person is important—critical to the success of your sale.

The sign checker checks on the status of the signs periodically while the sale is in progress. Sign checkers should make sure all the placards are still intact. If the originals have vanished, they'll need to make new signs—so take the necessities along on the check; tape, poster board, and marker.

The merchandise is gone, leftovers are back in the garage . . . ahh, it's over. But wait, one more thing: Take down your signs. You want to stay on the good side of your neighbors and help keep your area clean. Plus, you can reuse them for the next sale.

SECURITY

No matter the reason given—to use the phone, get a drink of water, or whatever—don't let anyone in your house. It's not worth the risk. Seriously, do they really need to try on a pair of pants that only costs a quarter?

Keep all the doors to your home locked—the backdoor included. When your sale gets busy, criminals can slip in through an open door and make off with some of your belongings. Keep the key in your pocket or fanny pack. I know a family who was having a big sale out front. When they went inside, they'd discovered someone had come in through an open back door and stolen money and laptops.

Cover things in the garage sale you're not selling with blankets or drop cloths. Otherwise, you'll be telling folks all day long they're not for sale. My husband puts up a sign with string across the open garage door that says, "This junk stays." (I just love him!)

Never leave your money unattended. Have one person in charge of the bank or keep it with you in a fanny pack.

And pay attention to the money you are handed. Unfortunately, criminals are finding garage sales easy places to pass counterfeit bills. Just listen to what happened to Darlene. She had just finished a successful garage sale, and with money in hand, she and her daughter, Rhonda, headed to an Indian casino in Phoenix to try their luck at the slots. Once inside the casino, Darlene put a $20 bill into the automatic money receptor but it slid back out. She tried it several more times. No luck. Then she slid another $20 into the slot. Same thing. Frustrated, she took the twenties up to the cashier's cage and asked them to change the bills. That's when her luck took a turn for the worse. "They looked at them, called the manager over, and then they told me, 'We need to see you in the backroom.' And that's when I thought, 'Uh, oh. Something's not right'." What wasn't right was Darlene's money. It was counterfeit.

Casino security snapped her picture, questioned her, and left her in a panic. "I was hysterical because then they called police in," she said, certain her next stop would be a jail cell. After four hours of interrogation, Darlene finally convinced the police she wasn't a criminal—just an unlucky garage saler who had the misfortune of accepting some bogus bills. "To think that anyone at a garage sale would even think of passing a counterfeit bill is disappointing," Darlene said.

Don't let a counterfeiter ruin your sale by leaving you with funny money. Here are some tips to avoid getting stuck with the fake stuff. Be leery of people with big bills—$50s or $100s. This is a garage sale! Buyers should be giving us small bills and coins. Anything larger than a $20 should raise a big red flag.

Be aware of a disruption—maybe someone breaks something, screams, or falls. Crooks often work in teams or groups. One or two will vie for our attention which can distract us from the "real" problem—someone else paying with a fake bill.

Business supply stores sell pens or markers that check the authenticity of money. Use it on the bill and if the mark turns an amber/gold color, it's the real thing. If the mark stays black, the bill's a fake. Be warned though, counterfeiters sometimes print large denominations onto real $5 bills. The pens won't work if you receive one of these fake bills.

Look closely. Does the bill look real, odd, or smaller? Is the print darker or lighter? Police say question it. Go with your gut. If it doesn't seem right, don't accept it. And, safety first. If you suspect a bill is fake, don't confront or accuse the "buyers." It's not worth getting hurt over a few dollars. Instead, here's what you do: Be polite and simply tell the buyer you don't have the change. Remember, if people are so cruel as to pass fake money at garage sales, who knows what they'd do if you point fingers at them. Then discreetly get their license plate number and consider calling authorities.

ATTITUDE OF GRATITUDE

When it comes to making money—the real stuff, that is— attitude counts. There have been times I have put on a sale when I've been grouchy and not exactly charming—yes, yes, even the Garage Sale Gal can get crabby, just ask my husband! And trust me, that crankiness cuts into the bottom line. It pays to just snap out of it! I try to have fun at my sales. I chat with people, listen with interest as they tell me about their favorite finds, and generally just have an all-around good time by showing my gratitude that they've walked up my driveway. Your sale will be a lot more enjoyable and successful, too, if you're in the right frame of mind.

2

GARAGE SALES

Buying Like You Mean Business

I've been garage saling nearly every weekend for more than a decade now. It's addictive. And, on those rare times I can't bargain hunt, I'm certain beyond a shadow of a doubt I'm missing out on the find of a life time. If I'm with my husband (who doesn't like to garage sale with me, saying I'm too "bossy"!) and I spot a garage sale sign, I simply must go. I mean it's a physical need—my heart beats faster, my mouth goes dry. So if he doesn't stop, I pout and give him the silent treatment until he— huffing and puffing and feeling defeated—

turns the car around. Works every time! And it's no wonder it makes me nervous to miss a day—the things up for grabs are nothing short of amazing. What if I would have missed the huge ornate wooden birdcage for just $5, the tiled-glass and iron coffee table for $10, which I later saw in the store for $475, and the 7-foot-tall iron candle holder I bought for $10? Garage sales are a never-ending, non-stop treasure trove of anything and everything you could possibly want or need. And these days—with the economy the way it is—it's certainly not hard to find them.

 **For the best selection, go bargain hunting early and on the first day. If price is what matters most, then go toward the end of the sale—some sellers even give things away.**

HOW TO BE A BUYER

As a buyer, getting a great price at a garage sale depends on two things: How badly you want something and how badly the seller doesn't. Many sellers know we like to haggle, so usually items are priced with room for negotiations. But some buyers aren't confident in their haggling skills and (gasp!) pay the marked price. Here are a few tips that'll help get you that 1960s, avocado-colored Easy-Bake Oven for a song. I never got one of those under the Christmas tree and I'm sure it stunted my cooking ability. As an adult—I kid you not—I've set my kitchen on fire while cooking, twice! Firefighters rushed to the scene both times. And when the fire captain told me I needed to clean my stove burners, I knew I wasn't cut out for cooking, or cleaning for that matter. So, I continue on my seemingly never-ending quest to find a classic Easy-Bake Oven. Hey, there's still hope for me in the kitchen!

BE RESPECTFUL AND FRIENDLY

Sellers appreciate a buyer who takes a genuine interest in their items—after all, it's their life lying out before you. Listen and you'll probably hear a wonderful story about that old metal mailbox. Be patient and you might end up getting an even better deal. This strategy only works, however, if you're sincere. If you don't care to hear their story, don't pretend—they'll see right through it.

Don't insult the sellers with such things as "this item certainly isn't worth $5" or "these sell for a lot less at other places." The seller might just tell you, "Then go to the other places." Remember, you want this item, so start off on the right foot.

"Is this your best price?" or "Can you do any better on the price?" is a non-threatening way to ask for a lower price. Plus, let the seller name the price and he may go lower than you would have.

If the seller holds firm on a price, then don't push it. You may want to pay the asking price. There are times I wish I hadn't been so stubborn—like when negotiating for a stained-glass window, an antique desk, and a nineteenth-century mantel clock. It was only after I left the sale that I realized they were already priced low.

 **Reality check: If that footed cake plate is marked $20, don't test a seller's intelligence by asking if he'll take $2. You'll probably offend him and that will get you nowhere. He probably won't even work with you on the price after such a low-ball offer. So, be realistic when haggling.**

JOIN THE DRAMA CLUB

Let's say you want a clock marked $10—chances are the seller will come down to around $8. If that's still too high for you, put the clock down and begin to move away from it. This is where your acting skills can come in handy. Pretend that price isn't even in your ballpark. This is a really good negotiation maneuver, but just be sure no one is lurking behind you ready to pick it up when you feign disinterest. If the seller wants to get rid of it badly enough, usually you'll hear something like, "What price would you pay?" That's when you know the ball's in your court. Tell them you only have $4 left. If it's the last day of their sale, they'll likely take it rather than put the clock back in the garage.

But remember, if it's the first day of the sale, the seller has another day to try and get rid of it, so your bargaining position is not as good and you might have to pay closer to the sticker price.

The fake out: I've never tried this, but it's been pulled on me—and quite craftily I might add. You and the seller agree on a price, but you would like an even better price. Pretend you don't have enough. For example, take a $15 footstool; you pull out your money and there's only $11. The seller sees you do this, so she's assuming you really are at the bottom of the piggy bank for the day. The seller probably won't quibble over the extra $4, and that night you'll be propping your sore, garage saling feet up on that $11 stool. If the seller stands pat on the price, go to your car and "scrounge" for change, and then pay the asking price. It seems a bit deceptive but it can help you save a few bucks.

 **Leave the Jaguar and Hummer at home—you lose all your bargaining power if you pull up in pricey wheels. I see this more often than you can imagine. If you can afford the nice ride, the seller concludes you can afford to spend top dollar at her sale.**

GOOD COP, BAD COP

I figured this out when my husband was along for the day—this was before he decided he didn't like garage saling with me. I picked up a vase marked $25 and asked if he liked it. He said, "Yeah, it's really nice." The seller heard this and I knew right away any bargaining power I might have had went up in smoke. When we left (without the vase), I explained to Kevin why he should have said he didn't like it. If he had done so, we might have had a chance at a better price. So, have one buyer express interest in an item, while her co-conspirator seems indifferent. You've got the "good" buyer who is positive towards an item and the "bad" buyer who isn't so impressed. The seller knows she has to lower the price or that "good" buyer won't leave with the item. It can be tricky to execute—but if a great price is your bottom line, it's worth a try.

FLAWS AND FAUX PAS

If you want an item but see a flaw—perhaps a chip or a missing part—make sure to point that out to the seller. Chances are they didn't see it when they were setting up shop and that can, and should, bring down the price.

Beware of the $1 faux pas. If something is under $1, pay it. Some people like to haggle no matter what the price is. Aren't those people annoying? Which brings me to the time I did it! In Indianapolis, while still new at this garage saling thing, I found a

1960s stained-glass Santa Claus candle holder. It was a quarter—25 pennies for heaven's sake! But the Garage Sale Gal just had to push it. I asked the seller if she'd take a dime. I'll never forget the look on that lady's face. She looked me up and down, rolled her eyes, and said, "Yeah, I guess." I handed over the dime. To this day, I regret doing that. I'd love to give her fifteen cents and apologize, "I'm sorry, I was so ah . . . frugal!"

THE GOOD PICKER-UPPER

As a buyer, if you learn only one thing from this book, let it be this: If you're at a garage sale and see something you like, pick it up and walk around with it! Even if you're not sure it's something you want, pick it up! I've learned this—and relearned it—the hard way. There have been many times when I've spotted a real gem, but didn't want to appear over eager, so I played it cool hoping to get a better price that way. Instead I walked away empty-handed.

➤➤➤→ INSPIRATION: When most of us arrive at a garage sale, our biggest challenge is usually deciding what to check out first from among all of the choices. Connie can't do that. She is blind. "It isn't really hard for me, but I've been blind all my life, so I don't miss things I've never done or seen." In 1967, Connie was two years old and playing in the basement of her family's home in Trenton, New Jersey, when she picked up an unopened bottle of root beer and shook it. The pressure caused the bottle to explode in her face. Today, Connie lives in Gilbert, Arizona. She's a busy wife and stay-at-home mom with two teenage sons and a house full of animals. Garage saling is her way of escaping the hectic household for some fun and relaxation. "It's great to get out and be moving around. I like the variety of garage saling and never knowing what you'll find." Connie hits garage sales with her husband, Pete, who guides her to things he thinks will interest her. "We've been garage saling together for so long that he knows what I like and don't like."

I met the couple at a garage sale where the three of us were pawing through about 200 wooden cigar boxes. They were beautiful with colorful vintage-style labels and various shapes and sizes. Pete would pick up one of the boxes, tell Connie the color, and then hand it to her so she could feel it. She would run her hands around the entire box, checking it like an expert cigar-box aficionado. "Usually I can catch something that people with sight can't. I can feel slight imperfections, if the label is peeling, or if there's a chip in it." Connie chose 60 boxes, paying a dollar each. She gave a few to her dad who "just likes cigar boxes" and the rest were put to use in her own home. She keeps receipts, bills, and other papers in them. The different-shaped boxes will keep her organized by helping her to know what each one contains—electric bills in the short fat box, receipts in the longer one, and so on. Connie, who is energetic and exudes positivity, has some advice for folks who may be facing challenges in their life, and for those of us who sometimes just have a bad day. "Don't sit at home and feel sorry for yourself. Get out of the house and do something with your life. You have to get over it. Be able to initiate your own training and know what to do to make your life better."

Ways to Avoid
My Mistakes

➡ Research before searching.

➡ Go into the trenches of a garage sale armed with information.

➡ Read books.

➡ Talk to antiques dealers.

➡ Check out the Web.

➡ Search for hairline fractures and cracks since that makes a difference in resale value, especially when selling to a serious collector who always wants items in mint condition.

➡ Magnify your finds. Don't be shy about pulling out a magnifying glass when you're at a garage sale to thoroughly examine items (though you will have "serious buyer" written all over you and may not get the best price). Maker's marks, dates, and other important identifiers on collectibles are important to read but they can be tough to see as they fade through the years.

DON'T DISCRIMINATE, GET OUT OF THE CAR

It's amazing what you can find at a sale that at first glance looks like it might be a waste of time. Earlier, I mentioned how I was able to make ends meet for a time by working the garage-sale-to-online-auction business plan. One of my favorite examples is the time I stopped at a ramshackle sale where things were strewn all over. Lying across one of the boxes was a limited-edition, leather Harley Davidson jacket. It was a rarity from 2003—the cycle company's 100th anniversary jacket. I paid $15 and sold it online for $372. I almost didn't get out of the car for that sale, but I'm sure glad I did.

GIFT GIVING

I buy gifts at garage sales and I'm proud of it. Nearly every garage sale I visit there are new things up for grabs. We've all received a gift that wasn't quite right or bought a dress one size too small certain you'd fit into it a month later and, sigh, you never did. Many months later it's gathering dust, taking up space, and makes you sick as you think of the money you spent on it. So, in the garage sale it goes.

One of my favorite brand-new finds is a Lenox bowl in the original box that I bought for $1. It was a gift that ended up in a garage sale. A woman was sitting in her driveway with just a handful of items for sale. The porcelain bowl, cream with hand-painted pink flowers, was in its original box with tissue paper. "Yeah, I got it as a wedding gift ten years ago and I've never even taken it out of the box," she told me. My lucky day!

BUY GIFT ITEMS AT GARAGE SALES

It's a great buying opportunity. I always pick up hostess gifts for next season. I typically pay about $1 to $3 for these items. I estimate about a third of what I buy at garage sales is brand new. Some of it I turn around and give as gifts, and yes, the receiver usually knows it. But since I'm the Garage Sale Gal, they don't seem to mind—at least that's what they tell me. Garage sales are great places to find joke gifts, too—perfect for gag gifts. I've come across "designer" toilet paper, and I can always find Chia Pets still in the box—you know those funny ceramic figures that grow grass? Things like this always get a great laugh and

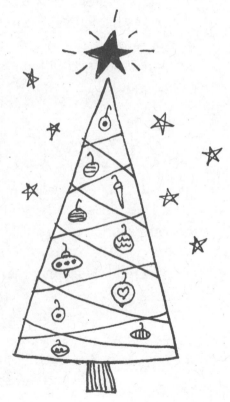

you can't beat paying a buck or two for this stuff. I also find brand new things that I can use for myself. I bought a pair of Burberry pants and blouse—$5 each and they still had the tags attached! I also bought a $50 yoga mat still wrapped in plastic at a garage sale for just $1. I still use it today. Namaste.

 Etiquette experts advise keeping secondhand gift-giving to ourselves. But the Garage Sale Gal disagrees—I say scream it from the rooftops! Garage sale gift buying keeps things out of landfills. We're repurposing, recycling, and saving money.

CHECK "NEW" ITEMS CLOSELY

I've bought things in original boxes assuming they were new only to find out they had been used. If it appears to be new in the box, ask the seller if you can take it out for a closer inspection. I once bought a cake plate, glanced at it in the box, and believed the seller when she said it was new. But at home, when I took my $3 purchase out of the box, I noticed scratches on it. I'd planned on giving it as a gift, but I sold it at one of my sales for $2 (I told the buyer it had been used). So, I lost $1 on the deal, but it was a low price for a valuable lesson.

MAKE A GAME OUT OF GARAGE SALE GIFT GIVING

For birthdays or any of the gift-giving holidays, set a goal with your family. Each person buys a new item at a garage sale to give as a gift. Set a price limit of $10—remembering the less you spend the better. You'll probably need to go to a few garage sales before you find just the right thing, but it can be fun.

I once even turned the gift-giving game into a television segment. I spent under $15 on gifts from garage sales and presented them on-air to the hosts of 3-TV's "Good Morning, Arizona." For one anchor, I found a set of six new-in-the-box, hand-painted champagne crystal goblets for just $3. They were handmade in Italy and, coincidentally, she had just returned from a trip to Italy. I found for the other anchor, who likes racing, a mini NASCAR race car for a quarter still in its original plastic packaging. For one of the newscasters, I purchased a cake plate and serving utensil in a beautiful box for $3. For another team member, an avid John Deere tractor collector, I found a small iron tractor painted yellow and green for $5. It wasn't brand new, but it was a collectible. And for the weatherman, I paid one thin dime for a joke gift that must have been purchased from one of those "As Seen on TV" commercials in the '60s—a pump to take the air out of food storage baggies. And it was unused, still in the original box! My total was $11.35. I then wrapped the gifts and presented them during a live broadcast to demonstrate

 Garage sales are great places to find gag gifts. I once picked up a plastic leg lamp (made popular in the classic movie *A Christmas Story*) for a buck at a garage sale and gave it as a white elephant gift.

that anyone can purchase great unused items at garage sales. Several of that 3-TV team no longer work at the station, but I'm absolutely sure they are still enjoying my gifts!

THE GULLIBLE GARAGE SALER

That's me!

If someone tells me a story about an item I'm admiring, chances are I'll believe it. I will usually buy a good yarn such as, "this platter is from the 1850s and belonged to my great-great-grandmother who treasured it," hook, line, and sinker—the item and the story! "It's a rare antique from Nebraska. It's been in my family forever," a seller told me referring to a trunk. I liked it and its history. So, I snatched up my "antique" trunk for the bargain price of $5. Problem is, I spotted a "replica" at a consignment store in Scottsdale. "Oh yeah, that's an old trunk, all right. Old Pier One Imports," the manager laughed, referring to the chain store. He told me it's not uncommon for owners to make things sound more intriguing than they really are in hopes of getting top dollar. But he, unlike me, is rarely fooled. "I do my homework. I shop a lot, keep my eyes open, and pay attention. You can learn a lot that way." I tend to make quick decisions about things I buy and usually that's a good thing, but not always.

I constantly need to remind myself to look more closely— for flaws, cracks, and fakes—and not get caught up in the moment. One time I bought a Ken doll that I thought for sure was priceless. The date on his lower back was 1968! Hardly able to contain my excitement, I happily shelled out $5 for Barbie's boyfriend. I was sure it would be a hot auction item since it was such an early version of Ken—which was launched by Mattel in 1961. When I got him home, however, I noticed Ken's head seemed a bit peculiar. So, I got out my trusty magnifying glass and examined his head a bit closer. Someone should have examined mine, too! The problem turned out to be a generation gap. Ken's head was from 1996. That new noggin on an old body rendered my "rare find" worthless. I've made other misdiagnosis, too. I bought Lenox porcelain manger-scene collectibles, only to get them home to find chips in the three kings, goats, and camels. I've also purchased "authentic" designer purses which turned out to be cheap knockoffs. I'm grateful for some of those bad choices of the past, however. They've forced me to be more patient and do my homework, which helps me to make better buys today at garage sales.

 If you're looking for furniture, carry a tape measure with you. If you don't have one, remember a dollar bill is 6 inches long.

DECORATE

Decorating a home with garage sale finds is a way to develop a personal style without the store and high price tag. If you're open to the possibilities, you can create a beautiful eclectic space. Furniture and decorator items are very common at garage sales. Sellers are always changing décor and they have to get rid of the old somehow. Here are ways you can see past the flaws and dust, and pick up some gems.

BE CREATIVE, UNIQUE

Unusual pieces are great for filling empty spaces in your home. I even buy stuff when I don't know what it is. I have a 3-foot, round, metal object on my wall which may be a table top, I'm just not certain. But it sure looks good hanging on the wall in the living room. I paid $3 for it at a garage sale in Carmel, Indiana. Another time, in Scottsdale, I bought three huge wooden picture frames for $4. I hung them in my really long hallway. They're empty—just the frames—but I love the green and brown color that decorates my once bare wall.

Old leather suitcases look great stacked together for a table or up on a shelf for added interest.

Reader's Digest books make great décor pieces. The leather-bound books with gold print look classy on a library shelf. I stack two or three to elevate plants, vases, and other objects d'art on tables.

Window glass blocks, usually leftover from remodeling projects, make for great decorator pieces. I pay about a buck for them—they usually go for about $20 in hardware stores. I also use these to elevate table items. On a serving table, place glass blocks in various areas, maybe two high in some, and throw a tablecloth over them. It makes for a great buffet table as the dishes are placed at different levels.

LOOK PAST THE FLAWS

Don't pass up an item that has a few problems. If I see potential in something that needs work—a table with missing parts, a lamp without its shade—I don't hesitate. Some of my best buys were eyesores or incomplete when I first spotted them, but with a little elbow grease, I was able to turn them into something I'm proud of today.

I once bought a 1920s farm table that had seen better days. Nothing but a smidgen of paint was left in several areas, leaving dried, gray-colored wood. The top was warped and had holes through it—I mean you could see the ground below if you were looking straight down on it. And three of the legs had rotted off. Despite all its imperfections, I loved it. What character! I paid $3. We fixed it up and today it has a prominent spot in the family room.

Another time, I bought an old table lamp made of real honest-to-goodness horseshoes at a garage sale in Scottsdale. It didn't have a lamp shade, the cord was frayed, and plugging it into a socket surely would have put some extra curl in my hair. But I couldn't resist the price, just $2! After rewiring it and buying a new shade, it sits in our entryway—on a garage sale table of course.

When it comes to buying garage sale items to decorate your home, throw out the rules. Think outside the box. And if you love it, buy it. You'll make it work.

3

THE PROS AND CONS OF PAWNS

When my publisher asked me to include pawn shops in this book I was, well, a bit befuddled. "You're kidding, right? Me in a pawn shop? I don't think so." Now, I didn't say that to her—if I did you wouldn't be reading this book right now. But, gosh, I've never been in a pawn shop in my life. The idea just didn't appeal to me. Thoughts of seedy, sordid, off-the-beaten path places always came to mind. But boy was my thinking skewed. And there were plenty of pawn-loving faithful willing to tell me how wrong I was. "A lot of people are like you and haven't been in a pawn shop. It's because Hollywood has vilified pawn shops.

Everyone thinks they're full of stolen stuff. Let me tell you, if that was the case, then don't you think the cops would shut us down? Pawn shops are just like every other business. There are seedy little places and then there are nice, clean, friendly pawn shops," says Rick, a pawn broker for 30 years. Marjorie, a middle class suburban mother of two, has always liked pawn shops. Her first pawn went down in 1987 in Altoona, Pennsylvania, when she sold an antique engagement ring for $1,400. "I couldn't believe it. I never dreamt I'd get that much for it at a pawn shop." Marjorie says she didn't even care if the ring was worth more. She was just happy to get rid of something her ex-husband had given her and make a buck at the same time. Since then, Marjorie has gone to pawn shops to sell, buy, and pawn. It's the first place she considers when getting rid of anything, no matter what the circumstances. "If my boys are misbehaving, I threaten them with, 'We're taking your games to the pawn shop if you don't shape up'." Marjorie says she'll always go first to a pawn shop when she needs some cash or wants to de-clutter because "it's just a lot easier than putting an ad in the classifieds."

Whether you're using a pawn shop to bring in money or to discipline the kids, it might just be the place for you to unload some of your stuff. The average customer is middle class, thirty-six years old, employed, and, about one-third are homeowners. Those of us who may need cash quickly and don't want to go through a credit check come from all walks of life. Even some businesses routinely rely on pawn shops to stay afloat. "We have a pawn shop here in Washington, D.C., that has been accepting pawns lately from restaurant owners. Times are so tough that the owners are pawning restaurant equipment and supplies simply to make payroll for the week," says Emmett Murphy, spokesperson for the National Pawn Brokers Association.

PAWNSHOPS ARE LIKE A BANK FOR SOME PEOPLE

According to a January 2009 survey by the FDIC, there are more than 9 million households in the U.S. who are "un-banked" or don't have a savings, checking, or any other kind of bank account. A pawn shop is the only place they can get a loan. Many of us depend on pawn brokers to help with small financial needs that we can't find at other institutions. For instance, most banks won't give you a $100 loan. Pawn customers are able to get short-term loans to cover unexpected expenses or help pay bills in an emergency.

The pawn process starts with the collateral—an item you allow the pawn shop to keep until you can pay back the loan. Let's say a customer brings in a DVD player and receives a 30-day loan of $80 (which is the national average pawn loan amount). By law, the pawn shop must hold the item for a set period of time—usually 90 days. In a month, the customer can buy back the collateral and pay the interest, which is on average 20% or $16. When the loan is due, if the customer can't afford to reclaim the pawn, he can choose to surrender the item to the shop, using it to pay back the loan. Or, if the DVD owner simply never shows up again, it then becomes the property of the shop. The pawn shop then marks up the price on the DVD player—usually doubling it—and sells it to recoup the money. One tactic that seems to be growing in popularity is re-pawning the same item over and over again. In a Las Vegas pawn shop, workers tell me one man continually brings in his daughter's laptop to pawn. He gets the cash, leaves the computer, then comes back in a week and pays off the loan. The man is happy, but I'm told his daughter is getting a bit frustrated. I would guess so!

Pawn shop owners will loan money for just about any kind of collateral, but the most common items pawned include jewelry, musical instruments, electronics, guns, and household items. There are thousands of pawn shops in the U.S. and in Canada, and most are mom-and-pop organizations. About 30 million people use pawn shops to obtain quick cash in the form of a short-term, low-interest loan. Pawn shops are governed under the same federal laws as any financial institution.

- -

 **More than 80% of all items pawned are re-claimed.**

- -

 In each pawn transaction, a valid driver's license must be presented and paper work signed. Each sale or pawn is reported to local law enforcement. This helps keep stolen merchandise out of pawn shops.

PAWN STARS

One place a lot of us can get a feel for how the pawn industry operates, and be entertained, too, is in a little shop in Las Vegas known as Gold and Silver Pawn Shop. But we don't have to go there; we can just turn on the television. *Pawn Stars* is a cable reality show about the pawn shop run by three generations of the Harrison family. There's Richard, the "Old Man," his son, Rick, "The Spotter," and his grandson, Corey, "Big Hoss." "The best part of the job is working with my family, and the worst part of the job is working with my family," laughs the jovial and personable show host, Rick Harrison. The show is funny, engaging, and informative as customers bring in unique things for the guys to evaluate and possibly buy. Although the show, seen on the History Channel, is about the pawn industry, most of what we see on the program are customers who sell stuff. There are two reasons for this—people who pawn (or go in for a loan) usually don't want to be on television and want to remain anonymous. (It's understandable; not many of us want to let the

Due Diligence for Pawning

=======================================

Check out the pawn shop with the Better Business Bureau. The BBB says pawn shop problems tend to increase in tough economic times because more people are using them. So make sure your shop doesn't have any complaints filed against it.

➡➡

Have an idea what your items are worth before you go in.

➡➡

Get a receipt.

➡➡

Get multiple offers on an item and you'll get the best deal.

➡➡

If you don't like the deal, don't take it.

⟫⟫⟩ → At the Gold and Silver Pawn Shop, Chumlee makes for great comic relief in the store and on the show. He tends to get blamed for everything, like the time two western cowboy dummies appeared in the store and Rick told him that was, "the stupidest thing you've ever bought." Turns out the "Old Man" bought them for $500. He liked them so much he even named them—Ed and George. Chumlee is a childhood friend of Corey's and "like a son" to Rick, but he's often the butt of all the jokes. He's also the one who gets to try out things that have been used for centuries, such as old rifles and other things that go boom!

world know we need help paying for a meal or paying a traffic ticket.) And, as it turns out, pawning doesn't make for good TV since most involve short-term loans for computers, printers, and other everyday items. But when people come in with things to sell, and Rick gets to appraise the item in order to figure out how much to offer the seller, well that's a different story. "It's something different every day. It's not assembly-line work. It's a challenge. It's a fun job. I've met everybody from billionaires to politicians. I get to see all walks of life every day." *Pawn Stars* is one of the most popular shows on cable television. So, I had to ask Rick, "Has your life changed with your newfound fame?" "It's changed a little bit. People are always asking for my picture. But I'm still a regular guy, still hang out with the normal people, and work is a lot busier now." Viewers aren't the only ones who like Rick Harrison, his peers do to. He was named 2010 Pawn Broker the Year by the National Pawnbroker's Association. Members say the overwhelming success of his show has "dramatically improved the image of the modern-day pawnbroker."

After being around the pawn industry for more than three decades, you can bet Rick has seen a lot of merchandise. One of his favorite things to come through the door is a sixteenth-century Italian painting of Jesus Christ. "An old man came in and said it had been left in an apartment he moved into. I paid him $2,000, but I told him it could be

worth more and we could get it appraised. He said, 'No, just give me the money'." Rick has yet to get it appraised, but knows it could be priceless.

So, I'm pleasantly surprised—whether you're buying, selling, or pawning—a pawn shop is a good place to check out. In fact, pawn shops are becoming so mainstream that more and more storefronts are opening in affluent areas such as Beverly Hills, Chicago, and Philadelphia. It's the new cool thing to do.

Most pawn shops now have websites where you can view items for sale. Checking the website is a great place to find out if the shop is right for you whether buying, selling, or pawning, and it's fun, too. For instance, in the Los Angeles area, the Woodland Hills Pawn Shop had a gorgeous yellow diamond ring for sale at a bargain price of $14,000. Now, if I could just win the lottery!

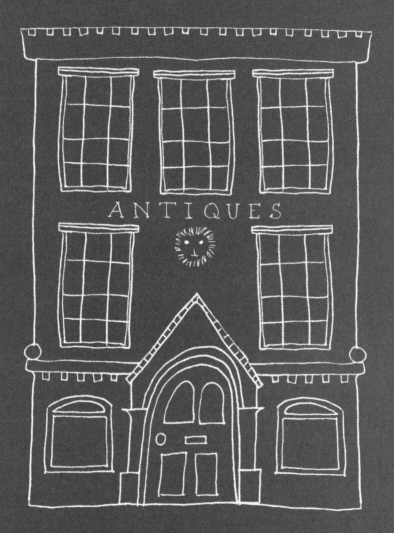

4

BE APPRAISED

No matter how or where you sell your things, whatever you do, make sure you know its value first. Imagine selling Great-Aunt Earlene's lamp for $10. You're thrilled because you were tired of looking at that old thing. But later your heart sinks when you find out auntie had more money than you thought and that lamp was a 1920s Tiffany worth $50,000! Ouch! That would be one lucky garage saler. (I'll keep dreaming!)

 **If you aren't sure of what you have, don't know its exact history, or just have a feeling about it—do your research!**

It 1971, in Estes Park, Colorado, Barbara benefited from someone else's mistake and discovered the find of a lifetime, along with a story she never grows tired of telling. She and her husband were at an estate sale run by the homeowner. Barbara had picked out some furniture and was paying the bill when she noticed some dinner plates stacked on a shelf in the garage. She went in for a closer look and realized what they were— antique flow blue plates. Flow blue china was made mostly in the 1800s in England and is known for its distinguished blue and white patterns. The seller's ancestors brought the plates over from England and her family used them every Thanksgiving. But the seller told Barbara she had always hated the dishes sporting a turkey in the wilderness. She had even overlooked pricing them for this sale, figuring no one would want them. She figured wrong.

Back then fair market value for each plate was about $30. Barbara knew she couldn't afford all twelve of them so she tried for just one. The seller declined, saying she didn't want to break up the set. Barbara, an avid flow blue collector, was walking away disappointed when her husband suggested she go back and see what the owner would want for all of them. "Well, I'd have to have at least a dollar a piece," the seller told Barbara. "I couldn't write that check fast enough. I was shaking so bad. I was so excited to get them for such a great price that I couldn't even remember how to spell the word 'twelve.' I had to ask somebody."

Later that day, now aware of her mistake, the seller called Barbara. "She tells me she wants them back. I said, 'No. A sale's a sale'." The seller then told Barbara she wanted six of them back. "And I told her, 'Sorry can't break up the set, remember?'." The seller gave up, but not before telling Barbara, "I hope you can sleep at night."

While the seller was crying "foul" over the turkey plates, Barbara slept just fine at night. Four decades later, Barbara still boasts about her discovery. "I cherish those plates. I believe everybody is due their one deal in life, their special little treasure they find, and this is mine. It's my best find ever—absolutely, I mean for a dollar a piece!"

Today those plates could fetch up to $300 each. But to Barbara, they're priceless and certainly won't be flying the coop anytime soon.

The seller in Colorado would not have made such a mistake if only she had done her own research or sought out the help of an estate sale company or appraiser. Which method is best depends on what you have and what you know or don't know. A gift, a family heirloom, a garage sale find, or even something you don't like should be appraised. You may not care for that tacky noisy cuckoo clock, but if it's worth $10,000, it's best to find out before you get rid of it.

DO YOUR RESEARCH

When I was talking to experts for this book, I asked each one to estimate the value of a Tiffany vase I own. (You'll see more on those results later.) What was the one thing each person had in common? The first place they all went to get a quick answer on the estimated value was online. So, that's the first step I'd take, too. Do a search for the item and see where it leads you. You will likely link up with sites that may have sold an item like yours in the past. You just might find the answer in a matter of minutes. But if you don't find something similar to what you have, this doesn't mean it isn't valuable. In fact, just the opposite— perhaps it's so rare no one else has it. Whether you find a match or not, try talking to antiques dealers about your item. Then if you still need more information, seek out the help of an appraiser. Make sure they're licensed and experienced. Two of the more reputable appraisal organizations are the

American Society of Appraisers in Washington, D.C., founded in 1936 and the oldest appraisal organization in the U.S. (www.appraisers.org) and the Appraisers Association of America (www.appraisersassoc.org). Both of these websites have information on hiring an appraiser.

APPRAISERS

Accredited appraisers will provide the value for fine and decorative arts, household items, jewelry, and much more. Fees vary depending on the service you want. If you have dozens of items and simply want a verbal appraisal, an appraiser will typically charge by the hour. If you want an appraisal on one specific item, in writing for insurance or resale purposes, the process is more involved. It requires research by the appraiser, who will then provide you with a written statement explaining what you have and how much it's worth. If your item turns out to be worth less than you hoped, at least you've done your homework and put your mind at ease.

Sean Morton, an antiques appraiser in Scottsdale, Arizona, has a few guidelines for getting collectibles appraised. If you have a mysterious item, get it appraised.

"Sometimes people aren't sure what they own or what it's supposed to be used for. And if they're getting ready to sell it or give it away, they might want to have it appraised first," Sean advises. And he says silver sets, paintings, and jewelry should always be appraised before liquidating them.

Ten years ago, in Fresno, California, Rick Norsigian was searching for collectibles at garage sales. He bought a couple boxes of stuff for $45—the owners wanted $70, but he was able to haggle on the price. Turns out the boxes contained sixty-five glass negatives created by Ansel Adams, the iconic landscape photographer. The images were believed

to have been destroyed by fire in 1937. Today, according to experts who spent months authenticating them, they are worth an estimated $200 million. Oops, not so fast. There are a few folks who say it's all a scam and the negatives belong to another photographer. There are several lawsuits filed against Norsigian trying to prevent the sale of prints. But, boy, if they are authentic . . . wow! It makes you queasy doesn't it? If only the sellers had looked more closely at what they'd had and sought out the help of an appraiser.

 **If you have rare items which might garner interest from a niche market, an appraiser can advise you on where it would sell best, at auction, to a dealer, or a collector or museum.**

5

AUCTIONS AND ONLINE SELLING ADVENTURES

When I lived in Indianapolis, I discovered the exciting world of auctions—the old fashioned kind at a place where the auctioneer runs the show. The auction preview itself, where bidders can examine the merchandise closely, is entertaining—a history lesson and a trip down memory lane all wrapped up into one. The first auction I ever went to was held in an old run-down barn south of Indy. I spotted a few things I wanted so I registered for a paddle number and settled in. I'm telling you I was so nervous you would think I was getting ready to perform a solo at Carnegie Hall. When the auctioneer pointed to "my" item—my mouth got dry, my palms grew sweaty, and my heart raced—I was now on deck. Would I get it? The competition was fierce but, not to be missed, I waved my paddle like I was guiding a jetliner to the gate. The last bid before the gavel came down was $60. "Is it mine? Did I get it?" I screamed out, praying I'd won the monstrosity. "Yes, my dear. The big iron pig is yours," the auctioneer said as people in the crowd chuckled. "That was my first auction-win ever," I gleamed to the people around me. Somehow I think they all knew that.

Eventually, I moved up in the world and found an upscale auction house that sold beautiful art, antiques, and collectibles. Yep, auctions were becoming old hat for this Gal, though there were still a few occasions when I thought my legs would give out on me, especially the time I ignored the high bids and kept raising my hand. It's hard not to get caught up in the moment. I won a pair of 1950s Baker chairs for $400, including the auction premium and tax. I immediately panicked, wondering if I'd over paid and if in reality they were the ugliest—or prettiest—chairs I'd ever seen. But when I got home, I knew I'd done the right thing. My husband loved them and immediately exclaimed, "They're Dick Van Dyke chairs!" He was right, they did look like something you'd see on that old show—the one where Mary Tyler Moore played his wife.

The thing about going to auctions as a bidder is that everything you buy becomes special. You remember the day, who you were bidding against, how you felt, and even how the place smelled—it's still a mystery to me, but the auction house in Indy always smelled like SweeTARTS (the candy in a roll) when you'd walk in the door. Maybe that's why I always had such a "sweet" experience there. But become the consigner, or seller, at the auction and it's not so memorable, at least not for me.

I realized the auction house was bringing in good money for each item, so I wanted a piece of the action—maybe I'd get rich. I brought in a huge antique J.G. Meakin white ironstone pitcher and bowl—the kind used in the olden days to wash up. I was certain it would bring in good money, but when the auction ended, I was disappointed. The winning bid was $60—the exact same amount I'd paid for the set at the Goodwill Store. I broke even, but still my selling career at auctions was over just as quickly as it had begun.

TRADITIONAL AUCTIONS

In a Dutch auction, the auctioneer starts with a high asking price and lowers it until someone bids. The winner pays the last price announced.

An absolute auction, or no-reserve auction, means there is no reserve or set price for an item or, in other words, there is no bottom price. An item could conceivably sell for $1 if only one person places a bid.

A reserve auction is an auction where the items have a

minimum bid that must be reached before they can sell. If they don't get the reserve amount, the item doesn't sell. Take Michael Jackson's Swarovski-crystal-studded glove he wore on his 1984 Victory Tour. It sold in the summer of 2010 for $190,000. This item wouldn't have sold unless it reached or went over its bottom price. According to the *Las Vegas Sun*, it was expected to fetch up to $30,000 but went far and above that when Wanda Kelley, of Los Angeles, bought it. By the way, she said she was willing to go higher.

Auction houses are good places to sell if you have a lot to offer or an extremely expensive and rare item. Upscale auction operations have a loyal following and spread the word about upcoming events so you can be sure the buyers will turn out in droves. I don't think my ironstone set got the affluent crowd aflutter!

ONLINE AUCTIONS

So, I moved on from the traditional to the online auction. The best thing I've ever done to make money at selling stuff was to buy low and sell high—go figure! I once bought two small antique-glass nursery-rhyme plates at a garage sale for a quarter each, put them up for bids, and got $52 for each one! Another time I bought a hideous (hey, it doesn't have to be pretty to be coveted) tavern liquor sign for fifty cents and sold it for $72. I bought an older, but authentic, Gucci shoulder bag for $1 and it sold for $132!

My re-sales sound pretty good, but are nothing compared to one of Steve's sales. Here's what happened. Steve bought some golf balls at a garage sale—three sleeves or boxes—each containing three Ping golf balls. The Gilbert, Arizona, resident hooked them for $1.50 and put them up for auction online at a starting price of $9.99. Within minutes, Steve knew these weren't just any golf balls. Bidders began offering good money for him to end the auction early, but he turned them down and let the auction play out. He then did some research and discovered the never used golf balls were extremely rare. They had been part of a special order placed by an Arizona church back in 1976. The purple and gold balls were one of Ping's first batches—before they began producing golf balls to sell at the retail level. Finally, with mere seconds left in the auction, bidders pushed the price up to $780. But in the world of online auctions, a lot can happen in the last few moments. In just 16 seconds, 26 more bids came in, propelling the ending price for those nine golf balls to $2,413.88! "When I saw the winning bid, I thought I was going to faint," Steve said. He got into the online selling business when he decided to turn a lifelong hobby of collecting into everyone's lifelong desire to make money. He left the banking industry to sell full-time on eBay and it seems to be working out. He brings in about $65,000 a year just by going to garage sales and selling stuff online. Nice gig if you can get it—and you can if you have the motivation!

Like Steve, selling things online can be an ideal way to be your own boss. It's also great if you just want to get rid of the clutter around the house or bring in money while in between "successes." All you need is a computer, a camera, and some merchandise. If you're not computer savvy—have no fear. I'm pretty darned computer-challenged, but even I can create online listings. Like anything, it just takes some time getting used to. Start small—I started with some Monopoly coffee cups. I had four of those game board mugs which I sold one at a time. My

Whether you're buying, selling, browsing, or researching prices, online auctions are a wealth of merchandise and information. They're a great place to buy and sell and learn about collectibles.

first one went to the highest bidder in Canada for $10. What a thrill! Here I had something just gathering dust around the house and I made a few bucks on it—very rewarding!

EBAY

eBay is one of the most widely used online marketplaces. It was launched in 1995 by computer programmer, Pierre Omidyar, who wondered what it would be like to sell things to people around the world. So, he created the computer code and listed a broken laser pointer. It sold for $14.83 to a collector. Today $2,000 dollars in goods changes hands every second on eBay.

OTHER ONLINE AUCTIONS

But eBay isn't the only game in town. There are dozens of online auction sites including eBid.net, onlineauction.com, uBid.com, and Bidz.com. Each has different fees and rules. Some have multiple charges related to just one listing—for instance there's a charge for each item listed whether it sells or not, a charge for a percentage of the selling price, for pictures posted and/or even a membership fee per month or year. Read the fine print to determine which site is best for you. You can also visit www.online-auction-sites.toptenreviews.com. This site rates the top ten online auction sites.

ETSY AND OTHERS

There are also specialty auction sites such as igavel.com and Rubylane.com which offer only antiques. Do you like to make things—jewelry, quilts, knitted clothing? Then maybe Etsy.com is for you. This site sprouted up in 2005 and caters to sellers who have a talent for making things. Listings can remain on the site for as long as four months at a cost of just twenty cents per item. Etsy gets 3.5% of the sale price, minus the shipping charges. You're allowed to sell crafts, craft supplies, and vintage items that are at least twenty years old.

IS IT HARD TO DO?

Most online sites make it very easy to sell. Remember, they want you to learn the ropes—the better you do, the better they do. Each auction site typically offers tutorials that show you step-by-step how to set up an auction. Once you get the hang of it, it'll be old hat to you. Like any business, the more time and effort you put into it, the more you get out of it.

Some sites also have live chat help so that if you get stuck while in the middle of trying to list something, you have a place to turn for quick answers.

Brooke started selling online in 1998. "I had been a TV reporter and I needed to get rid of my clothes, and consignment stores weren't paying enough." The Los Angeles resident has been hooked on selling things online ever since. Today, Brooke is a power seller—meaning she sells a lot of stuff. These days she specializes in selling high-end (think Chanel, Gucci, and Fendi) clothing, purses, and shoes. She even consigns for a few Hollywood stars and their estates. She sold a diamond ring that belonged to the late actress Farrah Fawcett. "With the economy the way it is, you have to get people to come to your listings. You have to be a destination for buyers." Brooke, who wouldn't divulge where she buys her inventory, has no problem doing that. She makes her listings "pop" with good pictures, accurate

>>>→ Don't beat yourself up if you buy something and it doesn't sell. It's a great way to learn. Steve, the successful eBayer, once bought six new printers for $250. What he didn't realize was that the power connections were for European electrical outlets, not U.S. outlets. Because they're too expensive to ship overseas, he's stuck with them. "They're still sitting in my garage," Steve said. "They're oversized paperweights now." The lesson here is look closely at things you buy.

descriptions, and eye-catching titles such as "OMG-These Gucci shoes are 2die4." LOL, it gets my attention!

Barbara, who lives outside of Boston and works part-time at an upscale clothing store, says she started selling online with an excess of purses. "I started because my daughter was working for Kate Spade and we were getting these fabulous bags for next to nothing and I thought, 'you know I gotta start selling some of these'." Barbara has so many repeat customers to her online page that she's become friends with some—even swapping houses for vacation in New Zealand with one. She says buyers can also be more honest than most of us might think. She cites the time she inadvertently sent a $600 designer bag to a man in Turkey and an inexpensive pair of shoes to a woman in Italy. Problem was—it should have been opposite— the woman was to have received the purse and the man the shoes. But Barbara was able to get each buyer to forward the item on to the correct buyer. "I didn't speak Turkish and he didn't speak English, but by golly I got that guy to send that

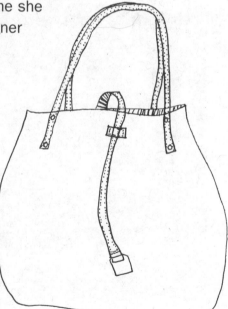

 Most auction sites keep the sellers honest by allowing buyers to rate their experience. The ratings or "feedbacks" help to weed out the bad or fraudulent sellers and it keeps the good ones chuggin' along.

expensive bag to Italy." On the flip side, Barbara says there are buyers who can put a damper on the process. She says they're the ones who are never happy with anything and can make it very unpleasant for everyone involved.

 Here's the beautiful thing about selling online. List an item and all you need is one buyer. Get two, and it's really interesting. More than one person vying for the same thing drives up the price.

WHAT TO SELL?

Looking for inventory? Chances are you're surrounded by it. Check your attic, basement, closet, or spare room. Something you stashed away long ago and forgot about may be a real treasure for someone else. Next, check other people's attics, basements, closets, and spare rooms—via garage sales of course—for additional stock. People are always selling things for a buck or two that might turn out to be a hot item demanding high prices online.

When deciding what to buy and sell, go with things you're familiar with. If you're a camera buff, buy cameras and parts. Expert in Franciscan pottery? Sell retired or hard-to-find pieces. Sell what you're familiar with and passionate about. Steve, the ex-banker, started with his collection of Matchbox cars and has never looked back.

Alison loves stuffed animals. So on weekends, she shops garage sales to build up her inventory, and during the week, she lists her goods online. The mother of three sells about sixty stuffed animals and other children's toys each week. It's paid off. She makes about $55,000 a year selling her garage sale stuffed animals.

TAKE A GAMBLE

If you see a bargain at a sale but aren't sure if it'll sell online, take the chance, as long as it's not priced too high. Even if the item is a dud online, you can always sell it at your own garage sale and make a profit.

CELL PHONE HELP

Technological advances are making it easier to prevent mistakes when searching garage sales for things to resell online. If you have internet access while you're out garage saling, you can check online auction sites before you open your wallet. One time I found a collection of twenty Walt Disney plates. The seller wanted $10 each and I was tempted, but not sure if they'd sell. I checked online and learned these plates were not in demand. I was able to save time and $200 by utilizing my phone.

KNOWLEDGE

Whether you know a little or a lot about collectibles, just get started. With every item you list, you'll gain valuable experience that'll help in your next auction. Try to buy things for your online inventory that you don't see everywhere else. If there are thirty pairs of Laurel Burch socks up for grabs from different wholesalers, you'll be lucky to sell them in your auction. So, go to garage sales with an eye for finding things that no one else has. Bottom line, it'll help your bottom line.

TOOLS

You need two must-have items to sell online—a computer and a digital camera. Make sure you take clear pictures of the item from several different angles. The more pictures you post, the more likely it is you'll get bidders to jump in on the auction action. If there are just one or two shots, a potential buyer may think you're hiding something. So, take pictures of the bottom of that silver Tiffany (can you tell I love Tiffany!?) candleholder and several close-up pictures from each side as well as any flaws it may have.

Garage sales are great places to buy low-priced inventory. Anyone can go to a store and buy a designer purse for $300 and hope to sell it for $350. The key is to find something rare, pay very little, and watch your auction price go up and up! Sold!

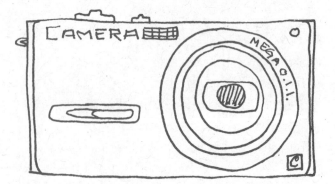

One final note regarding selling online. If you just don't have it in you—you don't have the time to sell online, get someone else to do it for you. There are store-front eBay shops or trading assistants in many cities that will do it for you. Customers drop off the goods and the business does everything—takes the pictures, lists the item, and ships it. They cut you a check minus their commissions and other charges, of course.

6

ESTATE SALES

The High-Brow Garage Sale

I f a garage sale is the compact car then an estate sale is the Cadillac of sales. An estate sale means you're selling everything, liquidating an estate—the entire contents of a home—not just furniture because of a décor change or the kids have outgrown their clothes. The homeowners need to sell their "estate," or home and everything in it.

The reasons for an estate or tag sale (as they're called in the East) vary, but the most common include a death in the family, a move to a nursing home or assisted living, divorce, or foreclosure.

If you believe an estate sale is the right route for you to sell your stuff—try tackling the project with the help of family and friends. Many of the same rules we talked about in the garage sale chapter apply to estate sales, such as advertising, making neat and bright signs, and having a lot of bodies on hand to help with the crowds, sales, and heavy lifting. Just make sure you know the value of the items. You might come across things you haven't seen in forty years or for that matter—have never seen—so do your homework or get professional appraisals on things you're unsure about.

If, however, you don't want to take on such a huge project, don't feel bad. Most people seek help because of the overwhelming enormity of the project and the emotional aspects of it. Estate-sale companies are run by pros who know collectibles and antiques. They are experts on art, jewelry, antiques, and other valuables. If they don't know about your specific items, they know who to turn to in order to get things priced fairly and accurately.

HIRING AN ESTATE SALE COMPANY

Anastacia Siembieda runs Angels in the Attic Estate Sales in Phoenix, Arizona, and has conducted more than 300 sales. She says although homeowners aren't required to be at the home the day of the sale, they should feel welcome and even encouraged by the estate company to be there. "If a homeowner is not welcome at the estate sale—then that's a red flag. That means they don't want the homeowner to see the price of items or the cash changing hands and the company may be hiding something."

Although you'll likely raise more money per item than you would at a garage sale, remember, in the end, the estate sale company gets a percentage of the profits. Rates vary but the average is about 20–35% going to the estate sale company. It can be well worth the price though, since as one estate sale

 **Most agents in the industry will work hard at your sale. After all, the more money they bring in the more they'll make.**

What to Do

➡ Find an estate sale company in your area on the internet or in the phone book.

➡ Check with the Better Business Bureau—experts say this is one of the most important things to do since this is where complaints—if there are any—are leveled against a company.

➡ Get free written estimates from three or more companies.

➡ Get references from past sales they've conducted.

➡ Make sure the company is bonded and insured.

➡ Make sure you see their plan for advertising.

➡ Find out how many people will work the day of the sale. There should be at least four workers or more depending on the size of the sale. A person should be at each door, the cash register, and at least one person should be assigned as a floater, a person who goes from room to room watching the activity.

➡ Get a contract in writing with all the details you've discussed.

➡ Get receipts and documented sales information at the end.

company owner told me, it's a turnkey process, meaning the company does everything—from digging your stuff out of closets and cupboards to pricing and staging your sale to cleaning and donating the leftovers to charity when it's over.

BUYING BASICS AT ESTATE SALES

If you like garage sales, chances are you'll love estate sales. Antiques store owners, collectors, and other re-sellers shop estate sales for their inventory, but you don't have to be a professional to attend; anyone can go. If you see an ad online or a sign, check it out. And there's no need to knock. This may not be common knowledge to first-timers, but it is okay to go ahead and open the door. Just make sure you have the right house! You'll likely pay more for items than you would at garage sales because of the quality of merchandise and work that goes into having an estate sale. The inventory, which is usually in very good condition, is cleaned and meticulously examined and researched before the price tags are attached. If an item has a defect, it's noted on the tag, such as "chip on rim," "lid missing," or it may simply say "as is." A flaw usually lowers the price of an item. But remember, estate sale workers are only human. It's possible they could miss a chip or scratch, in which case you can ask if they'll lower the price.

If you see something you like, pick it up and carry it or take it to the cashier. A lot of times workers will allow you to create a pile as you shop. If it's big—a chair, a couch, a desk—take off the price tag and hang on to it until it's time to check out. An item with a missing price tag means someone else has already beat you to the punch. But double check with the workers just in case the tag simply fell off.

While garage sales are all about dickering on prices, estate sellers typically won't negotiate on the first day of a sale. The second and third days are a different story, however. Operators are much more willing to come down on the price. The less they have to haul off when the sale's over the better.

If you live in a state where a sales tax must be added to estate sale merchandise, don't be surprised if you find that tacked on to your bill. Reputable estate sale companies have to play by the rules.

Estate sales have become so chic and popular that some less-than-scrupulous sellers are trying to cash in on the idea. Some people call it an estate sale when in reality they've simply opened up a store in a house. I visited one where the professional sellers had an entire walk-in closet full of brand new bedding still in original packaging. And the prices were higher than what you'd pay at the store!

But find a true estate sale and you will get some seriously smokin' hot deals, and memorable ones at that. In Indianapolis, I picked up an old round wooden footstool for $3. A few years later, during my marathon "Lucy" watching days, I saw the same stool in an *I Love Lucy* episode—one in which she and Ricky moved to the country and she was buying new furniture. That stool is the only thing Lucy left the store with. I'll keep that stool forever now! At another estate sale, I bought a 3-foot-tall silver-colored molded plastic rooster—wall hangings like this were popular during the 1970s. I paid $7 for it, and I'll never forget what a family member said to me as I was leaving the sale. "That was my aunt's favorite thing in this whole house. She cherished it. I hope you will too." Oh, I have been. I painted it red and it makes a great focal point on the wall above our kitchen table. Everybody comments on it. I love roosters and pick up antique and unique pieces whenever I can. My passion for them started on my grandma's farm in London, Ohio, with a 1950s cookie jar that sported a crowing rooster—which today is also in my kitchen, I'm happy to say. In Sedona, Arizona, I found a framed and signed rooster pencil drawing for $90. I know, sounds expensive right? But it's been appraised at $600. So, if you can find an honest-to-goodness estate sale—go in and check out the history, get a deal, and create some memories of your own.

7

ANTIQUE AND CONSIGNMENT BOUTIQUES

Speaking of memories—walk into an antique or consignment store and you'll take a trip down memory lane. It's especially endearing to visit one with an older loved one. Visiting a store with creaky wooden floors and shelves filled with things from yesteryear can be eye-opening. "Lynda, we had one of these when we lived on the farm." I can still hear my grandma telling me about the old phone—the kind where you had to pick up the base to speak into and hold the other part to your ear—we saw in a consignment store in Gatlinburg, Tennessee, when I was 10 years old. Both types of stores are stocked mostly with used items, but in a consignment store you'll find newer items while antiques stores are typically filled with more valuable and collectible items. By definition, an antique is an object one hundred years or older and is something often passed down from generation to generation.

ANTIQUES

I used to think antiques were just musty smelling things tucked away in an old person's attic. I still do, but now I'm the "elderly" person and they're in my home. Okay, I may be a few years away from getting my AARP card but I do have some interesting relics—like two architectural Rookwood pottery cornices from the entrance of an old building, a 1940s apothecary jar, two Louis Comfort Tiffany bronze compotes, and perhaps my favorite—an extremely huge leather, wood, and iron trunk once owned by the CEO of a clothing company in New York City. I also have my share of glass and ceramic candy compotes. I try and imagine where those decorative pieces have been, who owned them, and who might have reached their hand in the dish for one of those round pink mints with the wintergreen flavor—my grandma loved those and always had them handy in a bowl on a table by the television. The history, mystery, and romance is what drive a lot of us to keep searching garage sales, flea markets, and antiques stores for that rare and perhaps valuable collectible.

Diane has loved antiques since she was a little tyke. While growing up in Minnesota, her mother would buy old things, fix them up, and sell them to antique stores for a good profit. "She could take anything, no matter how bad it looked and clean it up and make it look wonderful. She was an inspiration to me." Today, Diane is following in her mother's footsteps. She finds all of her inventory at garage sales, fixes it up, cleans it, and sells it in an antique mall.

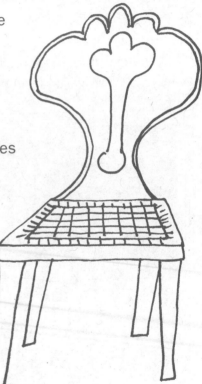

"Even on the bad days when there aren't many garage sales, it's fun." She snaps up books, golf clubs, purses, jewelry—even rabbit tails— and anything else that's unusual or unique enough to catch her eye. Diane began selling things in antiques stores for one simple reason, she needed an outlet. Because of her love for buying bargains, she had run out of room in her house and something had to give, but it wasn't going to be the shopping. "I love garage sales. It's like a treasure hunt. And now the antiques booth gives me a reason to continue my hobby. And I'm still having fun."

Diane is one of the lucky few, she makes money—not much, but at least, like most antiques dealers, she's not losing it. According to Greg Farr, manager of the Mesa Antiques Plaza, statistics show only 3% of people in the antiques business make money. Greg, who oversees about 100 antiques booths in his mall, says if you're thinking about renting a booth, you better adore antiquing because unless you run across an undiscovered Picasso, you won't get wealthy. And you have to put some elbow grease into it. "It's a full-time job. You can't just come in once a month and leave it at that. You have to change your booth often to keep it looking fresh and new." Greg says there's a fair amount of turnover in renters at his mall because people come

>>>→ Miriam Haskell, born in 1899, opened her first jewelry store in New York City in 1926. She created pieces that were popular among society women for years, including Lucille Ball and Joan Crawford. The line was, and still is, made entirely by hand. The company continues to be one of the leading makers of costume jewelry. A branch of the Haskell Company now manufactures and distributes Gwen Stefani's jewelry line–Harajuku Lovers.

in with high expectations. In fact, Diane says she's had booths in six different antiques malls since 2000, but was forced to find a new place each time a mall went belly up.

Prices vary from city to city for antiques booth rental, but to give you an idea of the costs, I'll share with you what Diane pays in the Phoenix area. She is charged $180 a month to rent two booth spaces. If she makes a sale, 10% of it goes to the store, and if the customer pays by credit card, she's charged a 2% processing fee. In March 2010, Diane had her best month ever in sales. She sold 66 items and brought in $800, but took home only $340. "I was really excited about making a profit, even if it was small. But this is no way to make a living, this is a hobby." Normally she says she's lucky to break even.

For Pamela, antiques didn't quite thrill her when she was younger. She grew up in an antiques store—seriously! Her mom operated one from their Houston, Texas, home and sold by appointment. "When I was a kid, I hated it. I wanted my house to look like the Brady Bunch house—the modern furniture and clean lines. We just had all this old stuff," Pamela told me.

Pamela's parents shopped together at garage and estate sales and other places where they might find something unique. "My mom used to look for antiques everywhere—even the trash. I was horrified." But in the mid-80s things began to change when, sadly, her father died. Pamela wanted to spend more time with her mom, and the best way to do that was to go antiquing with her even though she wasn't really into it.

But to her surprise, Pamela eventually started to enjoy the treasure hunts. She remembers one estate sale in particular that had a profound effect. She bought three pieces of Miriam Haskell vintage jewelry for just $2 each. When she sold two of the necklaces through an antiques trader's newspaper (one of the only places to sell at that time) and made a $100 she was hooked. That's when Pamela's mom told her she'd been "bitten by the antiques bug."

Today, one of Pamela's prized possessions is something that once belonged to her mother. It's a cookie jar by American Bisque. The ceramic elephant, dressed like a sailor, now proudly sits on Pamela's kitchen counter in her Austin home. "For the longest time, mom had that in her kitchen and I wanted it so much. I loved that thing. I kept asking her if I could have it." Finally, after years of begging for it, the cookie jar was Pamela's. Its estimated value is $120, but of course, for Pamela, it's priceless.

Pamela's mom died a few years ago, but she proudly continues the family tradition. "That is one of the hardest parts today when I'm antiquing; I think, 'Oh, Mom would love that.' I really want to share things with her, but I do feel like I'm carrying on her legacy now by antiquing. I guess you could say I've come full circle."

Today, Pamela's life is all about antiques; she writes about antiques and collectibles for the website: www.about.com, she has written a book, *Buying and Selling Antiques and Collectibles on eBay*, and sells on the website: www.Rubylane.com which specializes in antiques and collectibles. Pamela also co-founded Costume Jewelry Collectors International (CJCI), a club for collectors of costume jewelry, and serves as co-editor of the CJCI's quarterly magazine.

Now you figure since a lot of Pamela's life revolves around antiques, she would head to the antiques mall to unload her things, but that's not always the case. Pamela uses just about every venue you can imagine, explaining that where you sell your stuff all depends on what it is you're selling. If it's bric-a-brac or furniture, she likes to hold a garage sale. With antiques, Pamela does her research, finding out everything possible about the item. Then, perhaps she'll set up a table at a flea market to see what kind of response she gets on the item. Or, she'll try selling things to an antiques dealer. As for rare and hard-to-find or expensive items, she usually lists it on eBay. If it's costume jewelry (one of her passions), she likes her display case at the antiques mall. She's even found buyers for some of her things on Craigslist. "I really like it because it doesn't cost anything. I like selling where I can make the most amount of money and spend the least to get it sold."

Craigslist classifieds has had its share of crime-related activity. In Washington State, according to Seattle television station KOMO, a man was killed simply trying to sell jewelry. Another man was tied up in his own home after advertising his television for sale. Chances are things like this never would have

Safety Tips

=====================================

Never give out your home address online.

➡➡

Do not meet in a secluded place or
invite strangers into your home.

➡➡

Tell a friend or family member
where you're going.

➡➡

Take your cell phone along if you have one.

➡➡

Consider having a friend accompany you.

➡➡

Trust your instincts. Profit is
important, but safety is paramount.

➡➡

Be especially careful when
buying/selling high-value items.

crossed your mind—and there's a good reason for that—you're not a criminal! Unfortunately, we sometimes need to think like one so we don't become a victim. But there are thousands of sales that take place every day with no problems at all.

 **If you turn to any classifieds, including Craigslist, to sell your stuff—be careful and use common sense.**

CONSIGNMENTS

Consignment stores are another option for selling your stuff. Clothing, furniture, and bric-a-brac are the more popular items selling on consignment. Here's a general idea of how most consignment stores operate. Typically you'll make an appointment to show your items. Make sure your things are clean, in good shape, and in season. Don't take shorts in winter and coats in summer. Usually workers will tell you on the spot what they will try to sell and you can take the rejects back with you. The store decides the selling price and after the item has been on the rack for a set period of time—one week or a month—the price goes down and continues to do so until it sells. If it doesn't sell, usually you'll be given the option of picking it up or allowing the store to give it to charity (which is a

>>>→ I have a friend who took three boxes of clothing to a consignment store and she was aghast to learn they expected her to put everything on hangers, price it (at their discretion), and hang it up. And worse, she did it! Four hours later, when she'd finished the job, she called and asked me if I thought she'd made a mistake taking her clothes there. I don't mince words so I said "yes." She should have left the store the second they handed her a few hangers.

decision you'll make at that first appointment). Generally you'll receive anywhere between 40–60% of the selling price.

If you are looking into consignment stores, shop around for the one that's right for you. Make sure you choose a reputable store that has been in business more than three years, is a place you'd like to shop, and has a good location and track record of paying their consigners. I've heard stories about sellers not getting a dime and being told their merchandise was donated to charity. I've also experienced it first-hand. I won't mention the store by name, but I can tell you I dropped off clothing, mostly designer suits from my days as a TV anchor—they seemed

Consignment Checklist

➤ Chose a reputable store.

➤ Find a store in a good and safe location.

➤ Look at how the goods in the store are merchandized. Would you want to be a customer?

➤ You should receive monthly statements.

➤ Make sure you understand how the pricing works.

➤ Determine when and if your items go to charity from the start.

➤ Sign a contract that specifies terms and sales percents.

➤ Co-ops aren't as mainstream as consignment stores, but take a look and you just might be able to find one near you. Whichever venue you choose—antique booth, consignment store, or co-op—just remember, seller beware. And if the store is a good fit, put your heart into it, along with your attention and time, and it will pay off!

pleased with all of it, and said it would likely sell. A month later I went in and all I received was a check for $9 and no clothing to take back. They said they had given the non-sellables to charity. Alrighty, then! My advice would be to keep close tabs on your merchandise if you hand it over to a consignment store. But I guess that kind of defeats the purpose of consigning, doesn't it?

As for furniture, some stores want you to bring in the merchandise. It would be quite a hassle, however, if you arrived with your couch only for them to say no thanks. So, before you load up that four-piece sectional, make sure it's something you know they will be interested in trying to sell for you. Some stores will pick up items for a fee between $50 and $100. But they won't deliver it back if it doesn't sell. Instead, it'll go to charity. No matter where you're consigning—get everything in writing and read the fine print.

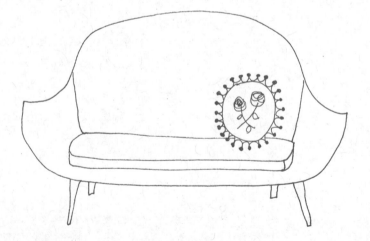

I don't mean to sound like a negative Nellie when it comes to consignment stores, but just be careful about which one you choose. The idea is to get rid of your stuff and make a little money, not create headaches for yourself.

CO-OPS

If you'd like to do that, and feel a bit like a store owner, then maybe a co-op or co-operative is for you.

Co-ops are similar to consignment stores but with one big difference—commitment. Co-operatives are a group effort—owners want you to not only sell your wares but also help make the store successful by working in it and/or donating your time for spiffing up projects.

With businesses closing, thanks to the economy, it's hardly been a good time to open a store. But that's exactly what Suzanne and a group of friends did in Layton, Utah, about 25 miles north of Salt Lake City. "We felt like there were a lot of other women in our area who are pickers, go to garage sales, and like to make stuff, but need help selling it in a different environment. And we thought, 'you know what, there isn't a cool store in Layton, so let's create one'."

>>>→ By the way, people who "pick" stuff are commonly referred to as "pickers." These treasure hunters love to go through old garages, attics, and such to find gems. In fact, there's a show on the History Channel called *American Pickers*. Cameras follow two guys who rummage through people's stuff and come up with some real dandies.

The result is a kitschy, fun shop that encourages creativity and revolves around family. The General Store is run out of an old bank building now listed on the National Register of Historic Places. "We cleaned it up and painted the walls bright colors . . . lime green, turquoise, and orange. People always come in and say 'this is really unique; I've never seen anything like it'. I remember, at the end of the first day, we looked at each other and said, 'we gotta get more stuff'," says Suzanne.

Members of the co-op are called "chicks" and pay $25 a month to sell their stuff. Each chick is also required to work in the coop a few hours a week. The store, with its eclectic mix of old and new, gets a small percentage of each sale as well. Buyers can pick up anything from vintage items, antiques and collectibles, to homemade clothing, and jewelry—one young "chick" makes earrings out of buttons. And then there are some things you might only see at the coop—like Chicken-Poop Lip Balm for $2.50. Sounds . . . ah, um . . . interesting?

The co-op seems to be a big hit since opening in the summer of 2009—with a line on the first day! The store continues to do a good business and has even turned a profit. People have come from as far away as Pennsylvania just to take a look . . . and probably pick up some of that lip balm!

 The Co-op Chicks' mantra: "One chick's clutter is another chick's cluck."

8

FLEA MARKET FUN

I remember when I was a little girl; I overheard my brother tell Mom he was going to the flea market. Why would he go to a market to buy fleas, I wondered? But a few minutes later, a little light bulb went off in my head. Ah, okay, he goes to the tackle shop to buy worms—so it makes sense he would head to the market for fleas.

When I got older, I discovered the flea market was a great place to find more than just "fleas." There are great deals to be found on everything from food, toiletries, and socks to art, antiques, and furniture and anything else you can imagine. They are a great place to make a quick buck, too. Flea market vendors are on the increase as we all try to bring in money from stuff we have around the house. "Business is great, it is way up. Guys are out of work, the wife's out of work, and they think 'how do we make money?' So they gather what they have and head to the flea market to sell it and make money," says Dennis Dobson, CEO of Canning Enterprises, Inc., which runs several California flea markets, including the world-famous Rose Bowl Flea Market in Pasadena. Dennis says flea markets always gain in popularity when the economy is weak. The lower prices attract more buyers, while the need for money attracts more sellers.

 **The Rose Bowl Flea Market, established in 1968, takes place every second Sunday of the month.**

HOW THE FLEA MARKET GOT ITS NAME

We can likely thank Paris for the name origin. *Le Marche aux Puces*, which translates directly to "market of the fleas," was so named by the French because of the flea-infested goods believed to be sold there. Back scratcher anyone?

> ⟫⟫→ The Paris Flea Market, launched in 1885, is billed as the largest antiques market in the world. Nearly 200,000 people visit the sale each weekend. Shoppers can find anything from antique furniture, architectural relics—think iron gates and stone cornices from old buildings—to post cards.

If the idea of selling your stuff from a flea market leaves you itching to get started, you don't have to go to Paris or Pasadena. Look for a place closer to home by perusing the yellow pages or internet. You can sell just about anything—save for illegal things such as firearms and pornography. Start with stuff sitting around your house. You will be surprised at what people buy: electronics, working or not (some people buy solely for the parts), buttons, fabric, handmade crafts, collectibles, furniture, and more.

WHAT TO DO

The biggest expense you'll have, aside from your time invested, is the booth space rental. At the Rose Bowl, prices range from as little as $25 a day for a small card table near the entrance to $250 for a 20-square-foot space, with the average running

Checklist
Before Choosing

- -

Find out the price.

➡➡

Find out the size of booths.

➡➡

What are the hours of operation—
are they open daily, weekly,
or once a month?

➡➡

Does the market allow for
one-time rentals? This is especially
important if you're just cleaning
out the garage or attic.

$100 for a 10-square-foot spot—which is what most people with garage sale items choose. But every market will have different prices, rules, and hours. So, if you are interested in selling at a flea market, find out the details first, that way you can choose the best place for you.

Each state and city is also different when it comes to what is needed to legally start selling. In California, for example, vendors can set up shop two times a year at a flea market without obtaining a tax number, in other words without collecting taxes on your sales. But have just one more—a third one—and you will need a tax identification number so the state can get a chunk of your sales. Details like this are things managers at your flea market are more than happy to help you with. They want to make it easy on prospective sellers—the more vendors they attract, the more money they make. And remember, you will likely have to bring your own tables and chairs but hopefully, if business is good, you won't be sitting much.

Oh, sure, most flea markets consist of vendors who sell wholesale products and handmade items, but here's some good news—it is okay to be a once-in-a-while vendor. This means if your house gets cluttered and it's time to purge, at least you know you have another option rather than holding a garage sale. You might make more money at a flea market than at a garage sale because your stuff is exposed to more people, but keep in mind booth rental and all the work that goes into it—loading and unloading the goods, pricing, and staging items. So, go ahead and pack up that old record player, steamer trunk, and ashtray you're tired of looking at and head to the market to park it, mark it, and profit!

STREET SELLING

So, what if you can't spring for the cost of a flea market booth? Well, if you're like Bill, you opt to sell on the streets. He sets up shop outside a friend's corner store at a busy intersection in Mesa, Arizona. On his first day out, he made $1,400. "I owned a crane company and I lost my business. I needed money, so I just set up here on the corner." Bill, who had been an antiques collector when his business was booming, was able to pay some outstanding bills with his intake. By the way, it is illegal to sell on the streets. Bill says he has been asked to move along by police, but usually he just takes his chances hoping no one will shut him down. I tried to contact Bill to get an update on how his sales were going, but unfortunately his phone had been disconnected—a sign of the times.

ALL THE WORLD'S A STAGE

Here's a radical idea for selling on the streets—but this is legal. If you're adventurous, want to take a road trip, and don't mind squeezing in among thousands of other sellers, then check out The World's Longest Yard Sale. It is 675 miles long, winds through several states along Highway 127, and stretches from West Unity, Ohio, to Gadsden, Alabama. Vendors sell everything from antiques to homemade goods, to garage sale items.

In 1987, Tennessee resident Mike Walker came up with the idea for the big multi-state sale. "It's a crazy, funny event. You have professional antiques dealers in one booth selling upscale items and then your neighbor selling old clothes in the booth next door. It's an incredible variety of things for sale." Mike was the Chief Financial Officer of Fentress County at the time and he and his staff brainstormed on ways to give tourism a shot in the arm. "We needed to bring people off the main interstates and into our area, and we thought this was the best way to do it." Mike credits childhood memories for helping him to come up with the idea. "When I was growing up, we had garage sales all the time. And Mom always took us to sales looking for bargains. So, yes, I love garage sales." Mike's mom, Carolyn, has a prime spot for the big sale. Her home sits right on the main stretch of Highway 127 in Tennessee. "I just love it. This is a great time of year." She usually makes about $3,500 during the event. Carolyn says she goes to garage sales throughout the year, buys items, and then resells them at the "Longest" sale.

If you go to buy, bring your patience. Mike says traffic moves at a snail's pace, maybe 10 miles per hour as folks look at merchandise from their cars.

Prices for renting a space vary from state to state, county to county, and even city to city. Private homeowners, businesses, and other property owners can charge vendors whatever they want—but they do have to stay competitive.

THE "WORLD'S" ADVENTURE

It was the adventure of a lifetime. Yvonne of Chandler, Arizona, and her best friend, Donna of Indio, California, were searching for bargains on Highway 127 in Tennessee along the "Longest" sale. There were so many sales that they were only able to travel 60 miles in the four-day trip. "The sales were right there on the road, right smack dab on the side of the road. It was so crowded it took an hour sometimes just to drive one mile."

They had flown to Alabama, so their stash had to be small enough to fit in a suitcase. They bought jewelry, books, and decorative items including a 2-foot-tall metal rooster sculpture Yvonne found for $30. She says she was thrilled with the buy—that is, until she went a few more miles and saw the same sculpture at another sale for just $15. Ouch!

While the sales were the main attraction, Yvonne says there were other things that made the trip worthwhile—the scenery, which includes mountains winding through quaint small towns, lakes, and lots of trees. And then there were the locals. "I just loved listening to the people. I loved their accents. And everyone called us ma'am. They were very polite."

Though they barely made a dent in the huge chain of sales, by the end, they'd had enough. And Yvonne says she hopes she never sees that many port-a-potties again in one trip!

The World's Longest Yard Sale begins the first Thursday of August and runs through Sunday. This sale is the most widely known, but others continue to sprout up around the country. Simply search online for "highway sale" and you'll get plenty of choices—maybe even one near you.

Whether you take a road trip or drive a few miles to the local flea market, just make sure your inventory consists of stuff you simply can't find anywhere else. For buyers, decisions are often based on emotion and memories, and as a seller, if you can evoke those feelings in a customer, you just may make more money than you ever dreamed possible.

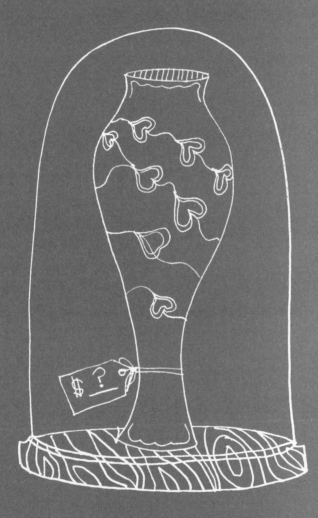

9

THE TIFFANY VASE EXPERIMENT

I bought a new-in-the-box Tiffany & Co. vase for $25 at a garage sale in Hawaii—yes, even in paradise I garage sale. I believe at the time the vase was selling for almost $100 in the Tiffany stores. It's a pretty ceramic vase with a bamboo motif, yellow glaze on the outside, and the famous Tiffany robin's egg blue on the inside. It's eight inches tall, in mint condition, and comes with the original

Tiffany blue box. It's never been used—it appears to have been a gift. I was certain I would double my money and it would sell quickly, but no such luck. (I was surprised, I mean it's Tiffany!) I sent pictures of the vase to some of the sources in this book to find out where I might get the most money. But remember, this is just an example. Everything you auction, sell, consign, or pawn will be different.

ANTIQUE SHOP/MALL

Diane says she would put a price tag of $40–$50 on the vase in her antique booth. She says the exact amount would depend on what she paid for it. "The best part of the piece is the name. The fact that it is new might make it less desirable. I would hope for a buyer to come by my booth that is impressed with the name and collects Tiffany. To move fast, it has to be a great deal and the right person has to see it."

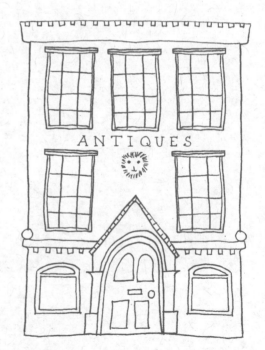

ANTIQUES

CONSIGNMENT STORE

Antiques expert Pamela says since it's a new Tiffany, she wouldn't hope for much since antique Tiffany sells better. She'd expect to net $25–$30. "My experience tells me this vase would do best in a high-end consignment shop where the "blue box" and Tiffany & Co. name are easily recognized by shoppers. And an antique store with a clientele interested Asian antiques might provide a good opportunity as well, since this bamboo motif blends in with that type of decor."

ESTATE SALE

Doris runs estate sales in Peoria, Arizona. She says at one of her sales she would likely put a price tag of $25 on the vase. If it didn't sell the first day, it would go down to half price on the second day of the sale.

PAWN SHOP

The place I got the highest "offer" or estimated selling price was at the place I figured I'd get the least! Imagine that. "Even though it's newer, I'd still give you $75 for it because I mean it's Tiffany, and Tiffany always sells well," says Rick Harrison of Gold and Silver Pawn in Las Vegas. Rick says he'd likely turn around and sell it for $150.

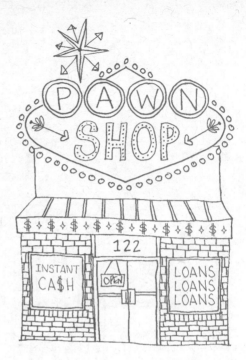

EBAY

I listed the vase twice on eBay at $69.99 and it never sold. I never even got any interest, which was surprising to me. I did see another vase exactly like mine sell for $53. I guess if I want to get rid of it—I should lower the.

price, but I just don't think I can do it! And keep in mind when things don't sell on eBay you still pay for the listing whether it sells or not. So it's cost me about $7 just to see if it'll sell. Ouch! I now have almost $35 invested in it. So, I better hang onto it for fifty years and sell it when I'm in my nineties! Stay tuned—I'll let you know how that works out for me.

10

GO SELL IT!

So, you've sold the clutter around your house. Now you're ready to broaden your sales potential to include buying low and selling high. If you need ideas and motivation to start your selling career, look for inspiration. You'll find it everywhere if you just pay attention. Mine came from a washed-up career in television news and a passion for garage sales. Eight years ago, at forty years old, I knew I didn't want to work as a reporter and television anchor anymore, but I also knew I had to do something. So, I opened my eyes to the possibilities. And it's amazing what can get your juices flowing. Something seemingly insignificant—a comment from someone, a walk around the block, or even exercise—can inspire. I get a lot of my newspaper column ideas when I'm on the treadmill at the gym. It seems the faster I run, the more ideas I get. But, of course, most of my columns come from meeting people at garage sales and hearing their stories—many of them full of inspiration about how they got started or what they sold that sparked a love of garage saling in their life. Stephanie Meyer's idea came to her in a dream. She's the author of the romantic *Twilight* series of books which have been turned into movie deals and millions of dollars. And it all started in her sleep!

You can even find ideas at garage sales. I've heard countless stories of people who started a business based on a garage sale find—like the woman who buys old typewriters and uses the parts in her jewelry making business and a woman who buys old vinyl record albums and molds them into handbags—now that just might be a number one hit!

No matter what you do—whether you're selling stuff around the house, handmade quilts, garage sale items, or whatever strikes your fancy—look for inspiration by keeping your eyes and heart open to the possibilities.

Happy garage saling!

RESOURCES

MEET THE GARAGE SALE GAL

The Garage Sale Gal

www.GarageSaleGal.com

This is my site where users across the nation can list and look for garage sales, get my favorite tips on how to make the most money, read my columns, and even watch my television segments.

GARAGE SALES: SELLING LESSONS FROM THE PRO

Lynda Hammond

www.azcentral.com/members/Blog/LyndaHammond

This is where you can read my weekly blog on the *Arizona Republic*'s website.

Life Organizers

www.lifeorganizers.com/cm_articles/102_10_ways_to_declutter_ your_home_280.html
www.downwithclutter.blogspot.com

These two sites have more good tips for getting rid of clutter in your house.

Abduzeedo

www.abduzeedo.com/useless-junk-turned-creative-diy-products
This is a great site to help you get your creative juices flowing with some of those garage sale finds.

Ehow

www.ehow.com/how_5800107_out-stuff-worth.html
This site has some good tips on how to figure out the value of things you may own.

Bankers Online

www.bankersonline.com
Visit this site to know how to determine if a bill is real or fake.

Quote Garden

www.quotegarden.com
Attitude is important no matter what we're doing in life. If you need some inspiration, visit this site.

GARAGE SALES: BUYING LIKE YOU MEAN BUSINESS

The People History

www.thepeoplehistory.com/toys.html
This site talks about some of the toys we used to play with. This might be something to check if you want to buy old toys at garage sales.

Emily Post

www.emilypost.com

Being polite can go a long way at garage sales. I know I can always use a refresher from the Miss Manners of our time, Emily Post.

Regiftable

www.regiftable.com

When it comes to giving gifts we've bought at garage sales, it can be considered "regifting" in its finest form. Here's a website on the issue.

Earth 911

www.earth911.com/recycling

This is a great place to look for more tips on recycling.

THE PROS AND CONS OF PAWNS

Pawn Shops Today

www.PawnShopsToday.com

This is a good website to learn more about how a pawn shop works.

National Pawn Brokers

www.nationalpawnbrokers.org

This site gives information on pawn brokers across the nation as well as statistics regarding the pawn association.

Pawn Stars

www.history.com/shows/pawn-stars

If you want to learn more about *Pawn Stars* on the History Channel, visit this site.

The Better Business Bureau

www.bbb.org

The Better Business Bureau's website.

BE APPRAISED

The American Society of Appraisers and the Appraisers Association of America

www.appraisers.org

www.appraisersassoc.org

The American Society of Appraisers and the Appraisers Association of America are two reputable appraisal organizations that you can consult. To find an appraiser near you, do a search on your computer by entering "appraiser" and your city.

AUCTIONS AND ONLINE SELLING ADVENTURES

Auctus Development

www.auctusdev.com/auctiontypes.html

You can find out everything you need to know about auctions here.

Auctions

www.auctions.nettop20.com

This site shows the top 20 auction websites across the country.

eBay

www.ebay.com

This site will teach you how to sell your stuff and is also a helpful place to research the value of things.

Auction Guide

www.auctionguide.com

This is a great site to find any kind of auction (and type of auctioneer) you can think of . . . from livestock to land to memorabilia.

Other Good Sites

www.eBid.net, www.onlineauction.com, www.uBid.com, www.Bidz.com, www.igavel.com, www.Etsy.com, and *www.Rubylane.com* are all helpful sites for online selling and buying.

ESTATE SALES: THE HIGH-BROW GARAGE SALE

The Better Business Bureau

www.bbb.org/us/article/you-need-to-hold-an-estate-sale-where-to-begin-657

If you're planning an estate sale, check out the Better Business Bureau for some helpful tips.

Ehow

www.ehow.com/how_137449_successful-estate-sale.html

Visit this site for more tips on holding an estate sale.

www.ehow.com/how_2079829_buy-estate-sales.html

For tips on how to buy at estate sales, check out this site.

ANTIQUE AND CONSIGNMENT BOUTIQUES

Antiques

www.antiques.about.com/od/buyingandsellingantiques/a/aa050302.htm

This site has helpful tips for looking for antiques at garage sales.

Miriam Haskell

www.miriamhaskell.com

Visit this site to learn more on the history of Miriam Haskell jewelry.

Costume Jewelry Collectors

www.costumejewelrycollectors.com

Learn more about costume jewelry by visiting this site.

Sites for Selling Antiques

www.rubylane.com

www.Craigslist.org

These are common sites for selling antiques.

Ehow

www.ehow.com/how_108289_rent-space-antique.html

Tips on renting space at an antique mall can be found here.

Stretcher

www.stretcher.com/stories/990809d.cfm

This is a good place to find tips on selling your stuff through a consignment shop.

FLEA MARKET FUN

The Rose Bowl Flea Market

www.rgcshows.com

This site will help you find out more about the Rose Bowl flea market in Pasadena. It also has information on several other major area flea markets as well as everything you want to know about setting up shop in a flea market.

Paris Perfect

www.parisperfect.com

Visit this site for more on Paris flea markets. This site is geared toward apartment rentals, but it has a lot of good reliable information on the Paris Flea Market, including hours of operation.

Paris Logue

www.parislogue.com

This site has helpful tips on the dos and don'ts of flea marketing.

127 Sale

www.127sale.com

This is the site for the World's Longest Yard Sale. Their website includes information on how to set up shop during the week-long sale, maps, hotels, and restaurants.

Bargains Galore on 64

www.bargainsgaloreon64.com
Churches, schools, and families set up booths along a 160-mile stretch of Highway 64 in Arkansas from Fort Smith to Beebee. Check out their information.

US 80 Sale

www.us80sale.com
Find deals along scenic U.S. Highway 80. The sale starts in Mesquite, Texas, winds through Louisiana, and ends in Jackson, Mississippi, for 392 miles of sales.

GO SELL IT!

Thinking about making a change in your life? Here are a few sites that may give you inspiration:
www.wisebread.com/feeling-stuck-100-ways-to-change-your-life
www.zenhabits.net/7-little-habits-that-can-change-your-life-and-how-to-form-them
www.livingorsurviving.com

MY SUCCESSES

ITEM	PRICE PAID	SOLD FOR
Example: Chair	$10	$55

MY SUCCESSES

ITEM	PRICE PAID	SOLD FOR

NOTES

NOTES

NOTES

☞

NOTES

Lynda Hammond is the Garage Sale Gal. She turned her hobby into a full-time career, not only by generating an income from her garage saling habits, but by creating a website to help others sell their stuff—www.Garage SaleGal.com. She also writes a weekly column for *The Arizona Republic*, appears on local Phoenix and national television stations with segments on garage saling, and has even taught a course on the subject at a community college. Lynda, her husband, and their two dogs, Millie and Roxy, live in Mesa, Arizona.